THE
RIGHT BRAIN
MANAGER

THE
RIGHT BRAIN
MANAGER

*How to harness the power of
your mind to achieve
personal and business success*

Dr. HARRY ALDER

PIATKUS

First published in hardback in 1993 by
Judy Piatkus (Publishers) Ltd of
5 Windmill Street, London W1P 1HF

Reprinted 1994

First paperback edition 1994

Reprinted 1995

*A catalogue record for this book
is available from the British Library*

ISBN 0-7499-1226-X
ISBN 0-7499-1349-5 (Pbk)

Edited by Kelly Davis
Designed by Chris Warner
Set in Linotron Baskerville by
Computerset Ltd, Harmondsworth
Printed and bound in Great Britain by
Biddles Ltd, Guildford and King's Lynn

Dedicated to a coal miner and philosopher,
shipyard worker and historian,
patriarch and sage:
the late William Henry Alder.

CONTENTS

FOREWORD

THE BOOK you are about to read is a different sort of management book. It will require you to set aside many of your assumptions and preconceptions about your role as a manager, and go on a journey into hitherto unexplored reaches of your own mind.

As you will discover, your thoughts are the key to your actions and achievements in life. By taking control of your own mind, you can literally change reality.

However, in order to gain this control, you have to undergo a course of mental training, both theoretical and practical. This book provides the mental training you need.

As you read *The Right-Brain Manager*, you may come across unfamiliar terminology and exercises that seem far removed from your day-to-day duties as a manager. Nevertheless, if you persist, you will discover powers of creativity, imagination and insight you never knew you had – powers that will revolutionise every aspect of your life.

The human mind represents not just the greatest unexplored frontier of understanding, but an infinite resource for personal excellence. A new kind of manager is needed to meet the challenges and opportunities of a new millennium – Manager 2000. You can be part of a thinking revolution that is set to change corporations, industries and societies worldwide.

1

A BETTER WAY OF THINKING

THERE IS NOW AMPLE EVIDENCE that what makes the difference between mediocrity and excellence is the *way* we think. Management is a thinking business. The best managers do not boast physical prowess, but they can outsmart and excel in how they think. One thing we can be sure of is that we all have infinitely more brain power than we are ever likely to use. It has been calculated that your memory could acquire eleven new facts every second of your life for more than seventy years and still have ample storage space in reserve. Yet many people mistakenly blame limitations in brain capacity for poor performance. How often have you heard the expression 'my brain can't take it all in'? It can. The secret is in learning how to access its enormous creative and memorising abilities.

Personal and management effectiveness is largely to do with the way you think but it is also to do with how you feel. Sometimes you just seem to be fated to have a 'bad day'. Feelings, attitudes and beliefs go on inside, beyond the reach of your conscious thinking and control, and are not included in the management textbooks. Yet they can often account for enormous variations in human achievement. Those moments when your unharnessed brain comes up with the goods – a flash of inspiration, an answer out of the blue – are all too rare. Unlike the latest trading account or an analysis of strengths and weaknesses, they refuse to be called up at will.

In order to utilise more of our mental power we need to find out how our brains work. The fundamental fact to understand is that we actually have two brains – almost identical separate halves, joined together with some communication fibres, but otherwise operating quite independently, and in entirely different ways. The right side is the seat of imagination, insight and vision. The left side is concerned with step-by-step logical thought, and language. Because the left side has traditionally been seen as the home of orthodox, rational thought, and is guardian of the language we have come to depend on for all such thinking, it has become known as the dominant side. Western education and professional training is therefore very biased towards the left brain – so much so that the imaginative right brain has all but atrophied in many adults.

In recent years we have come to understand a lot more about the mysterious, belittled right brain. And at the same time we have begun to discover a new and better way of thinking, using the whole brain. This new kind of thinking offers enormous potential benefits in every aspect of our lives, both personal and professional.

In this book, my primary aim is to enable you to find out more about the workings of the right brain so that you can harness its extraordinary power in your day-to-day life. In the course of this exploration, we will cover some familiar subjects – imagination, memory, creativity, self-image. In particular, we will try to get to grips with those eureka moments, those flashes of insight that can bring instant solutions and uncanny creativity. But the first step is to familiarise ourselves with the brain as 'a piece of hardware'.

The general purpose computer

The human brain has been described as the only general purpose computer that can be run on glucose and made entirely by unskilled labour! Unfortunately it is also the only computer that is delivered without an instruction manual. So we have to learn as we go along.

Back in 1946, R. W. Gerard, writing in *Scientific Monthly* on the brain and the imagination, commented that it was sad but true that most of our understanding of the mind would remain as valid and useful if, for all we knew, the cranium was stuffed with cotton wadding!

More recently, comparisons with cybernetic systems, such as guided missiles, robots and computers, have given us some insight into the workings of the brain. But as each new marvellous revelation is unfolded, it only serves to underline how much more we still need to discover about this enormously complex organ.

Maybe if it were simple enough for us to comprehend, the human brain would be too simple to permit such comprehension! But over the years the brain has been investigated through its anatomy, psychology, ethology, biochemistry, neurophysiology and biophysics. More recently the brain's electrical activity has been measured with increased accuracy and sophistication, as scientists have 'watched' the processes of thought – with no idea, of course, of the nature or content of those thoughts.

Because most of its workings are still so mysterious, we have tended to resort to similes and analogies when discussing the human brain. Descartes, the seventeenth-century philosopher and mathematician, likened brain function to hydraulically operated statues in the gardens of the royal palace at Saint-Germain, writing of a 'reasoning soul' in the machine. By the early twentieth century the favourite simile

3

had become a gigantic telephone switchboard. Not surprisingly, the digital computer won the contest in this half of the century, and by the early eighties experts were likening the brain to a network of interconnecting computers, each with its own highly specialised function, such as language, short-term memory, vision, hearing and so on.

Your unlimited brain power

Apart from its amazing complexity, it is the sheer capacity of the brain that defies description. A show-stopping comparison used to be made with the famous Cray computer, one of the most powerful in the world. That computer, all seven tons of it, even when operating at 400 million calculations a second, would take 100 years to accomplish what your brain could do in a minute! These are facts that every harassed manager should take to heart. We need to work smarter rather than harder. We need to use more of these vast brain resources. And in order to do this, we need to get a better feel for the power of this three-and-a-half pound, grapefruit-size, singularly unattractive lump of grey matter – so that we can begin to *trust* its working. We need to be fully convinced that it has the potential to do any job we set it.

We can start by looking over the shoulders of the scientists who first put the human brain under the microscope. They found that each brain comprised millions of tiny cells called neurons. Then in a scientific saga akin to the birth of astronomy the scientists found that each of these cells had octopus-like tentacles radiating out from a central nucleus. It was then observed that these tentacles were covered with thousands of tiny protuberances, like the tiny suction pads on an octopus. By this stage it was estimated that the average brain contained 10,000,000,000 neurons.

At the same time, other researchers were trying to relate intelligence to brain size, but no such relationship was found. People with small brains were highly intelligent, and vice versa. Professor Pyotr Anokhin, the protegé of the psychologist Pavlov (of Pavlov's dogs fame), was among the first to realise that it was not the number of brain cells that determined intelligence but something to do with the little protuberances on the brain cells' tentacles. He found that each protuberance was connected to at least one other, and that by means of electro-chemical impulses these two could form little patterns with other individuals and other groups. He then realised that each brain was actually a fantastic interlinking of patterns formed by these billions of protuberances.

In the last year of his life, Professor Anokhin calculated the number of connections and pathways that could be made by a normal brain. He emphasised, as a scientist, that his estimate was conservative, and concluded his last public statement by saying he was convinced that no man was alive or had ever lived who had even approached the full use of his brain. The number he calculated is still staggering to the scientific and lay world alike. The number was *1* followed by *10 million kilometres* of standard typewritten noughts!

But that was only part of the story. It has since been shown that if the brain is stimulated, no matter at what age, *it will physically grow more protuberances*, thus increasing the total number of brain interconnections. And these new interconnections can be generated at a faster rate than the cells naturally die off. This is good news for the over-forties who for far too long have been led to believe that their brains peaked between the ages of eighteen and twenty-four, and were thereafter doomed to deteriorate.

The message from all this is very clear. Our potential as human beings is not limited by our age, the size of our brains, or any inherited physiological characteristics. We are all potential Einsteins or Da Vincis! The secret is in the way we *use* this fantastic personal resource. The hardware is standard. It is the operating software that creates what we think of as human genius, software that we can write and change *at will*.

With much less effort than you might expect, learning how to use your brain more fully can bring you management and personal success at a level as yet unimagined. But before we can apply these principles, we have to find out a little more about these twin sides of the brain.

2

IN TWO MINDS

ALTHOUGH THERE HAVE BEEN great scientific advances in understanding the two halves of the brain in quite recent times, there are plenty of clues in our language and culture dating back many centuries. The distinction between right- and left-handedness has historically had strong connotations, right being equated with good or strong, and left with bad or weak. The Latin for 'left' is *sinister*. It is only in recent years in our own culture that parents have not well-meaningly tried to force left-handed children to use their right hands. And there are many other examples of the lesser status we assign to the left hand — controlled as it is by the right brain.

'Split-brain' experiments

Nobel Prize-winning physiologist Roger Sperry and his colleagues can be credited with providing much of our present understanding of the physiology of the brain. Their famous 'split-brain' studies were based on patients who had undergone a surgical severing of the *corpus callosum*, the main communication link between the two sides of the brain, consisting of some 200 million nerve fibres.

Without the connecting fibres, the researchers found, each 'mind' functioned separately and had no idea of what was happening inside its partner. So, for the first time, they were able to study the separate functions of each side of a single human brain. Through sophisticated testing procedures, Sperry and his team worked to determine which tasks were performed by which side.

Some strange examples of brain function emerged from these experiments. For instance, a film of the first split-brain patient shows a manual 'battle' between the patient's two hands as each tries to carry out a test – each side of the brain thinking it can do better than the other. The left hand (controlled by the right brain) is adept at tests involving shapes and pictures, while the right hand (controlled by the left brain) is close to hopeless in this specialisation but will not submit to the other side, knowing neither its different way of thinking, nor the fact that it can do the job better.

So which side of the brain is called into use in everyday tasks? Sperry and his team found that in tests requiring a quick response, *whichever side got there first* furnished the necessary solution. In other words, when 'left to themselves' the right brain will respond more quickly to faces or visual images, and the left to words and language. Any slight advantage is magnified over time, however, as the dormant partner increasingly stands back to let the other side handle a certain kind of recurring task with apparent ease. Ideally, each side will do what it does best. In reality, it does what it *thinks* it does best. So bad habits can form, in which the wrong hemisphere prevails and prevents true abilities from being expressed. You and I cannot begin to overcome such bad thinking habits without an understanding of this dual working of the brain.

In 1964 Roger Sperry concluded decisively: 'Everything we have seen so far indicates that the surgery has left each of these people with *two separate minds*, that is, with *two separate spheres of consciousness* . . . each disconnected hemisphere appears to have a separate mind of its own'.

Apart from Sperry's actual research, there is plenty of evidence from the patients' later experience to confirm this staggering conclusion. For example, there was the man whose right and left hands struggled against each other as he tried to put on his trousers in the morning. The same patient, in an argument with his wife, grabbed at her with one hand, only to have the other hand come to her rescue, pulling the first hand away! A lady, in choosing clothes from her wardrobe, would reach for something with one hand, only to have her other hand come up and take something different. And what of the shop worker who was unable to stack cans on the shelves. No sooner had one hand stacked a can, than the other would take it down!

Although you and I are spared these embarrassments, having 'joined up' minds, they illustrate the fact that different thinking processes are simultaneously and, it seems, mutually incomprehensibly going on in the two hemispheres. Apart from the inner conflicts that seem to be a neurological fact of life, there is a positive side to all this. You have *two* minds to use – for solving problems, making decisions, and going about your day-to-day work. And like trusted members of a team, together they can think better, each seeing things in a different light. The key to quality thinking is this partnership of two minds in one person.

Right- and left-brain ways of working

By understanding the special skills of each hemisphere, you will be able to use your mental powers more fully, thus regenerating latent right-brain functions, and restoring the balance that should exist naturally. It is this balance that produces the best thinking, and will mean greater productivity and effectiveness in any sphere you choose.

When you are engrossed in an exciting novel, your imagination comes into play and you inwardly see and feel the characters, events and situations. This is where the right brain takes over. It deals in images and feelings. It is the right brain you should credit when you instantly spot a familiar face at a large social gathering. The right brain takes in a total picture, in an instant, and links this with your massive memory store of every face you have ever seen. The left brain might eventually, in some logical, sequential way, register acquaintance with the person across the room, but would be stumped if, for example, the man had shaved off his beard, or had changed his appearance through ageing.

The right brain is able to absorb a mass of data simultaneously through all five senses, and, without any conscious effort, produces meaning, or a solution. When you say, 'I've got a feeling I've seen that person before', the feeling comes from your right brain. Your dominant left side might argue that it is impossible – you may, for instance, be in a strange foreign town. But your right brain is usually right. 'Trusting your instincts' means trusting your right brain, the source of hunches and so-called feminine intuition.

The main distinction between the two sides is usually described as verbal–spatial. The right brain is able to understand shapes, places and distances well, and the left brain handles language and logical or sequential reasoning. Recent research, however, seems to have moved away from this functional division – what the respective hemispheres do – to *the way they do it*. Thus the left brain mainly operates *analytically* (one logical step at a time); while the right brain perceives *holistically*, or in parallel, lending itself to handling pictures, scenes, spatial relationships, and the feelings that these arouse.

Each side of the brain, then, primarily performs certain types of function, but within an intricate partnership arrangement. They complement each other in all sorts of ways, as can be seen in many displays of human achievement.

For example:

- The poet draws on the right hemisphere for deep feeling and vivid imagery, but the left side finds the words to fit those emotions.
- A manager will suddenly be aware of a solution to a difficult problem in a relaxed moment , but only after gathering and pondering all the facts using the left brain.
- An architect uses his or her right brain to form spatial and aesthetic relationships, but depends on the left brain to handle dimensions, stress estimates, and the details of building regulations.
- A scientist needs the left brain for deductive reasoning, but it is the intuitive right brain that often produces a leap of insight to solve the complex problem.

So we need to know our minds – both of them – and begin to harness them in ways that will bring about the goals we want to achieve. Nearly all our management thinking to date has centred on the left brain. We can now add right-brain thinking to create a winning partnership.

At this point, we can draw up a list summarising the main functions of the right and left sides of our brains.

LEFT BRAIN

Verbal: This side controls speech, and is able to read and write. It remembers facts, recalls names, and knows how to spell.

Analytical: This is the logical, analytical side. It evaluates factual material in a rational way.

11

Literal: This side only understands words in their most literal sense.

Linear: Information is processed sequentially, one step at a time.

Mathematical: Numbers and symbols are understood, allowing advanced mathematical calculations to be made.

Controls movements on the right side of the body.

RIGHT BRAIN

Non-verbal: This side works in images rather than words.

Holistic (or non-linear): This side can process many kinds of information at the same time, sees problems holistically, and can make great intuitive leaps. It is able to evaluate the whole problem at once. The right brain, for example, remembers faces, seeing the features 'as a whole'.

Spatial: Perceptions of space and location are handled by the right side. It allows you to do jigsaw puzzles, and stops you getting lost in town, or even in your own home.

Musical: Innate musical talent, and the ability to respond to music, is a right brain specialisation – although much of the hard work of musical training occurs in the left hemisphere.

Imaginative: This side can fantasise, make up stories, and knows how to play. It can ask 'What if?'

Spiritual: This is the side for worship, prayer and mysticism.

Dreaming: Dreams are primarily a function of the right brain.

Controls movement on the left side of the body.

Drawing with your right brain

A simple exercise illustrates some of these points. If you are a non-drawer, you might be pleasantly surprised at what you can accomplish through 'right-brain drawing'. If you are already a skilled artist you are likely to find the exercise even more illuminating. Read all the instructions that follow before starting to copy Pablo Picasso's sketch, *Portrait of Ivor Stravinsky*, shown on the next page.

The drawing will be done using your usual hand, but *upside down*. Picasso's sketch is shown upside down, and you should not look at it the right way up until the very end, or you will gain far less from the whole exercise. Never having seen Mr Stravinsky upside down, you will have to draw just what you *really* see. Here are the instructions:

1 Find a quiet place where you can work uninterrupted. Play relaxing music if you like. Finish the drawing in one sitting. It should take you about forty minutes – maybe more.
2 Look carefully at the upside-down drawing for a minute or two, seeing the way the lines fit together, the angles, intersections, and their relationship to the whole page.

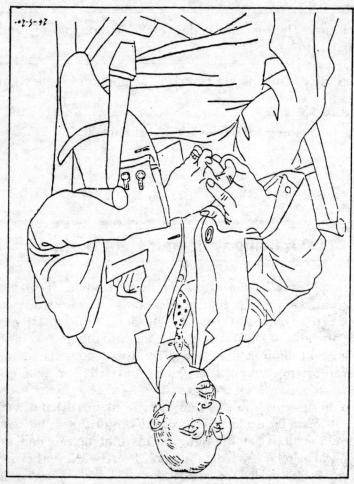

Drawing of Igor Stravinsky (1920) by Picasso
© DACS 1993

3 Start at the top and work down, line by line. Don't think about any of the man's features. He is not a man, just a collection of lines and shapes!

As you gradually work down, your left brain will have to switch off, as it will not find familiar patterns and concepts

14

(like a nose, arms and fingers). This is an easy exercise. Don't make it complicated. Just enjoy the experience of working in a right-brain mode. The whole image is right in front of you – nothing is missing. All you have to do is copy the shapes.

I hope you are pleasantly surprised at the quality of your drawing. If you practised regularly in right-brain mode you would soon become accomplished, and have a far better appreciation of art, and the skill of observation – which is sadly undervalued in management. Besides using your brain in a very different way, the right brain mode also changes your state of mind. So the whole exercise is a creative and therapeutic one.

The use of these right-brain drawing techniques ·is not confined to would-be-Picassos. It has been found to be a very helpful way of coaching managers and business people in right-brain approaches to problem-solving and creativity.

The Western left-brain bias

If you rely heavily on the left brain, and this is the main effect of our Western education and training processes, you may lose the intuitive powers of the creative part of your mind. Such an imbalance is bound to affect your overall abilities. It is now possible, by understanding this specialisation, and the different ways each side seems to work, to actually *stimulate* a specific hemisphere to fulfil a certain task, or address a certain problem.

In Western culture, a high value is generally placed on left-brain functions, while right-brain features tend to be neglected. At school we are praised for remembering facts and doing sums, but day-dreaming, a delightful indulgence of the right brain, is not acceptable. Left-brain dominance is also reflected throughout higher education and professional training; it is the source of so-called scientific method, and the rational thinking we have come to value so highly. In short, we are a left-brain society and we have suppressed the imaginative powers of the right brain. But these powers can be reawakened with simple exercises based on an understanding of the respective roles of these two sides of our brain. Just as your body responds to a well-designed physical exercise programme, your brain will rediscover its former strength and flexibility through a carefully thought-out programme of mental training.

Where do you fit on a right–left scale?

Before we start exercising our right brains in earnest, you may find it useful to assess your current mode of thinking. The following is based on a questionnaire which is often used at management seminars. It should give you a rough idea of whether you tend more towards the left or right side of your brain. Just answer the questions quickly and in-stinctively. Don't think about scoring until you have finished, and don't worry about whether an answer seems good or bad. There are no goods and bads or rights and wrongs.

Tick just one letter – the one that fits you the nearest, unless the question asks otherwise.

---

(1)   In a problem-solving situation, do you:

a.   Take a walk and mull solutions over, then discuss them?

b.   Think about, write down all alternatives, arrange them according to priorities and then pick the best?

c.   Recall past experiences that were successful and implement them?

d.   Wait to see if the situation will right itself?

---

(2) Day-dreaming is:

    a.   A waste of time.

    b.   Amusing and relaxing.

    c.   A real help in problem-solving and creative thinking.

    d.   A viable tool for planning my future.

---

(3) Glance quickly at this picture.

Was the face smiling?
  a. Yes.   b. No.

---

(4) Concerning hunches:

    a.   I frequently have strong ones and follow them.

    b.   I have strong hunches but don't place much faith in them.

    c.   I occasionally have hunches but don't place much faith in them.

    d.   I would not rely on hunches to help me make important decisions.

---

(5) In thinking about your day-to-day activities, which is most typical of your 'style'?

    a.   I make a list of all the things I need to do, people to see.

    b.   I picture the places I will go, people I will see.

    c.   I just let it happen.

d. I plan the day's schedule, working out appropriate times for each item or activity.

(6) Do you usually have a place for everything, a system for doing things, and an ability to organise information and materials?

a. Yes.   b. No.

(7) Do you like to move your furniture, or change the decor of your home or office frequently?

a. Yes.   b. No.

(8) Please tick the activities you enjoy:

☐ Swimming   ☑ Travel
☐ Tennis   ☑ Cycling
☐ Golf   ☐ Collecting
☑ Camping/Hiking   ☑ Writing
☐ Skiing   ☐ Chess
☑ Fishing   ☐ Bridge
☐ Singing   ☐ Roulette
☐ Gardening   ☐ Charades
☐ Playing an instrument ☐ Dancing
☐ Home Improvements   ☑ Walking
☐ Sewing   ☐ Running
☑ Reading   ☑ Hugging
☐ Arts/Crafts   ☑ Kissing
☑ Cooking   ☐ Touching
☐ Photography   ☐ Chatting
☑ Doing nothing   ☐ Debating

(9) Do you learn athletics and dancing better by:

a. Imitating, or getting the feel of the music?
b. Learning the sequence and repeating the steps mentally?

(10) When playing a sport or performing in public do you often perform better than your training and natural abilities warrant?

a. Yes.   b. No.

(11) Do you express yourself well verbally?

a. Yes.   b. No.

(12) Are you goal-oriented?

a. Yes.   b. No.

(13) When you want to remember directions, a name or a news item, do you:

a. Visualise the information?
b. Write notes?
c. Verbalise it (repeat it to yourself or out loud)?
d. Associate it with previous information?

(14) Do you remember faces easily?

a. Yes.   b. No.

(15) When you use language, do you:

a. Make up words?
b. Devise rhymes and incorporate metaphors?
c. Choose exact, precise terms?

(16) In a conversation, are you more comfortable being:

a. The listener?   b. The talker?

(17) When you are asked to speak off the cuff at a meeting, do you:

a. Make a quick outline?

b. Just start talking?

c. Shift the focus to someone else or say as little as possible?

d. Speak slowly and carefully?

---

(18) In an argument, do you tend to:

a. Talk until your point is made?

b. Find an authority to support your point?

c. Just become withdrawn?

d. Push the chair or table, bang the table, talk louder – shout?

---

(19) Can you tell fairly accurately how much time has passed without looking at your watch?

a. Yes.　　b. No.

---

(20) Do you prefer social events that are:

a. Planned in advance?

b. Spontaneous?

---

(21) In preparing yourself for a new or difficult task, do you:

a. Visualise yourself accomplishing it effectively?

b. Recall past successes in similar situations?

c. Prepare extensive data relating to the task?

---

(22) Do you prefer working:

a. Alone?　　b. Or in a group?

---

(23) When it comes to 'bending the rules' or altering company policy, do you feel that:

a. Rules and policy are to be followed?

b. Progress comes through challenging the
   structure?
c. Rules are made to be broken?

(24) At school did you prefer:

    a. Algebra?   b. Geometry?

(25) Which of these handwriting positions most closely
resembles yours?

    a. Normal right-hand position.
    b. Hooked right-hand position (fingers pointing
        towards your chest).
    c. Normal left-hand position.
    d. Hooked left-hand position (fingers pointing
        towards your chest).

(26) When taking notes, do you print:

    a. Never?   b. Frequently?

(27) Do you use gestures to:

    a. Emphasise a point?
    b. Express your feelings?

(28) Do you instinctively feel an issue is right or correct,
or do you decide on the basis of information?

    a. Feel.   b. Decide.

(29) Do you enjoy taking risks?

    a. Yes.   b. No.

(30) After attending a musical, can you:

    a. Hum many parts of the score?
    b. Recall many of the lyrics?

(31) Please hold a pencil perpendicularly to the ground at arm's length, centred in your line of vision and lined up with a frame, board or door. Holding that position, close your left eye. Did the pencil appear to move?

    a. Yes.   b. No.

(32) Sit in a relaxed position and clasp your hands comfortably in your lap. Which thumb is on top?

    a. Left.   b. Right.   c. Parallel.

(33) Tick the statements you feel are true about you:

- ☑ I can extract meaning from contracts, instruction manuals and legal documents.
- ☐ I prefer to work from diagrams and plans.
- ☑ I strongly visualise the characters, setting and plot of novels.
- ☑ I prefer friends to phone in advance of their visits.
- ☐ I dislike chatting on the phone.
- ☑ I find it satisfying to plan and arrange the details of a trip.
- ☐ I postpone making telephone calls.
- ☑ I can easily find words in a dictionary and names in a telephone directory.
- ☑ I love puns.
- ☐ I take lots of notes at meetings and lectures.
- ☐ I freeze when I have to operate mechanical things under stress.
- ☐ Ideas frequently come to me out of nowhere.

(34) I have:

    a. Frequent mood changes.
    b. Almost no mood changes.

(35) I am:

   a. Not very conscious of body language; I prefer to listen to what people say.

   b. Good at interpreting body language.

   c. Good at understanding what people say and also the body language they use.

SCORING

Here's the key to the self-assessment exercise. Circle the scores for each of your answers.

(1)	a. 7	**(2)**	a. 1	**(3)**	a. ③
	b. 1		b. ⑤		b. 7
	c. ③		c. 7		
	d. 9		d. 9		

(4)	a. 9	**(5)**	a. 1	**(6)**	a. 1
	b. 7		b. 7		b. ⑨
	c. ③		c. ⑨		
	d. 1		d. 3	**(7)**	a. 9
					b. ①

(8)

Swimming	9	Travel	⑤
Tennis	4	Cycling	⑧
Golf	4	Collecting	1
Camping/Hiking	⑦	Writing	②
Skiing	7	Chess	2
Fishing	⑧	Bridge	2
Singing	3	Roulette	7
Gardening	5	Charades	5
Playing an instrument	4	Dancing	7
Home improvements	3	Walking	⑧

23

Sewing	3	Running	8
Reading	③	Hugging	⑨
Arts/Crafts	5	Kissing	⑨
Cooking	⑤	Touching	9
Photography	3	Chatting	4
Doing nothing	⑨	Debating	2

(9) a. ⑨
b. 1

(10) a. 9
b. ①

(11) a. 1
b. 7

(12) a. 1
b. ⑨

(13) a. 9
b. 1
c. ③
d. 5

(14) a. ⑦
b. 1

(15) a. ⑨
b. 5
c. 1

(16) a. ⑥
b. 3

(17) a. 1
b. 6
c. ⑨
d. 4

(18) a. 3
b. 1
c. ⑦
d. 9

(19) a. 1
b. ⑨

(20) a. 1
b. ⑨

(21) a. 9
b. ⑤
c. 1

(22) a. 3
b. ⑦

(23) a. 1
b. ⑤
c. 9

(24) a. 1
b. ⑨

(25) a. ①
b. 7
c. 9
d. 3

(26) a. 1
b. ⑨

(27) a. 2
b. ⑧

(28) a. 9
b. ①

(29) a. 7
b. ③

24

(30)	a. 9	(31)	a. ⑧	(32)	a. 1
	b. ①		b. 2		b. ⑨
					c. 3

(33)	Contracts	①	Postpone	7
	Diagrams	7	Find words	①
	Visualise	⑨	Puns	③
	Advance	②	Notes	1
	Chatting	3	Freeze	3
	Plan trip	①	Nowhere	9

(34)	a. 9	(35)	a. ①
	b. ①		b. 7
			c. 5

Now add up the number of points you have scored and divide the total by the number of questions you have answered. (This latter number will vary, since questions 8 and 33 have a large number of parts.) If your points total 300 in 40 answers, for example, your final score would be 7.5, revealing a definitive tendency towards right-brain thinking.

1	3	5	7	9
Left				**Right**

3

SENSE AND SENSIBILITY

JUST AS WE CAN EASILY develop bad habits (perhaps when driving a car or handling the filing in the office) so we can easily slip into inefficient ways of thinking. We therefore need to find out more about *how we think*, so that we can begin to take control of our thought life, and bring about change for the better.

A good place to start is with the five senses, which are the basis, not just of what we experience, but of what we think and how we feel. Through these senses we have learned to survive in the world. We have nothing else on which to rely. We have come to depend on these senses; we *believe* what they tell us.

But any manager who has faced problems of communication knows only too well that individual perceptions can differ widely. Sometimes people see and hear what they *think* they see and hear, and no amount of argument can change what they think. Clearly, it is not what we see through our eyes or hear through our ears, but what is recorded in the brain that is important. What we *think* we see is, quite simply, our reality.

From electro-chemical brain reactions, based on information from our five specialised receptors – our senses – come 'understanding', 'experience' and 'consciousness'. And these relate to thoughts about the past, present and future. Thinking is the manipulation of these inner recordings of the five senses. This is how otherwise meaningless light and sound waves are transformed into real, tangible things that make sense to us. And this is how countless billions of colourless, lifeless, random bits of energy can be experienced as glorious sunsets, familiar faces or favourite puddings.

Back to the future

What happens when you recall something? You recall the same sensory perceptions as the original experience recorded. You access that part of the brain that recorded, electro-chemically and permanently, its interpretation of the energy waves processed at the time.

And what about the future, when you imagine what may take place, sometimes very vividly? You use the same inner senses to picture, or hear or feel what you think will happen. In each case, you are using your inner senses to create your own reality. Your brain cannot differentiate between what you usually think of as objective reality – the external, material world – and clearly imagined images. Through tiny electro-chemical recordings on the cortex of the brain, both produce what we refer to as *consciousness*.

This is how you can begin to use your thinking powers to change first your inner reality, and then (because they always follow) your external behaviour and achievements. You can create your future by learning to create *your own reality*.

Put your thinking skills to the test. Try and recall the face of a school teacher, as far back in your school life as you can go. Visualise the person clearly. Then recall the sound of his or her voice, the sound of the chalk on the blackboard, the echoing voices in the school gymnasium, and whatever other sounds come to mind in re-living that school situation. Then try to recapture feelings, sensations – the wooden surface of a desk, the feel of a cold shower. Allow yourself to be absorbed in the memory and your thoughts will flit from one inner sense to another, re-experiencing past reality. In doing this, you are successfully locating specific memory recordings filed away along with billions of others, and mentally re-living that past experience.

But the mind is not limited by past or present reality. You can imagine more or less anything. What would your boss look like in gigantic Wellington boots? Imagine an over-turned bus in front of your house. Imagine what it would feel like to climb the last few stairs of a skyscraper. In each case you readily employ thought processes that reflect all the senses in a real life situation. These inner senses are the very stuff of the mind as it remembers, ponders and imagines.

You can decide what to think

Learning to control your thoughts in this way can bring enormous practical benefits. To start with, you can decide what to think – what to remember, what to imagine, what to dwell on, and what not to think about. Subjective thoughts, unlike so much of the objective external world, are within your control. If a past experience gave you pleasure, then recalling that experience will bring with it that same feeling of pleasure. The more vivid the memory, combining as many of the senses as possible, the more the feeling of pleasure will be recaptured. You can test this easily by watching a friend, with their eyes closed, recalling such a pleasant experience. You may see their shoulders begin to drop, taking on a more relaxed posture, and a faint smile might be seen – the whole physiology responds to what is happening in the mind. Medical tests would also show a change in their blood circulation, breathing rate and overall metabolism. And all this is accomplished in moments, *simply by thinking*, without artificial stimulants or depressants, and regardless of circumstances.

As well as recapturing positive memories, you can derive benefits from imagining future events. If you have to undertake a task which makes you feel uneasy or anxious – perhaps something that you find very distasteful – you can choose to imagine the best rather than the worst. Apart from the therapeutic effect of positive imagining, as opposed to health-damaging worry, your actual performance in the real situation will be improved. The element of the 'unknown' will have been taken care of (repeated imagining has the effect of making the experience familiar), and you will have mentally associated the event with pleasure rather than pain, thus overcoming the negative association.

As we have already seen, the brain cannot tell the difference between present senses (what is actually, objectively happening) and clearly imagined or recalled thoughts. For this reason, when waking suddenly from a vivid dream, you are sometimes momentarily unsure whether you are awake or dreaming. Both worlds seem equally real. There is no difference in the way you feel, and the intensity of the experience your brain records. Similarly, when daydreaming, there is a time gap in your conscious, objective world – you are simply not aware of what is going on around you – and that gap is filled by the inner, but just as real, subjective world of your mind. So the objective material world and the inner subjective world become *one world* of consciousness, understanding and personal reality, drawing on the same raw material – the five senses.

Your world is different to mine. Our personal 'maps' of reality are not the 'territory' of the material world, but our unique, sometimes distorted representations of it. And therein lies the key to a myriad so-called communication problems that beset managers at every level and in any culture.

So using your senses means much more than being observant and alert to what is going on in the material world. It means harnessing your thought life to bring about real changes in how you feel, how you perform, and what you accomplish.

Learning to use your thinking skills

Automatic skills, like driving a car, first have to be learned, and that requires plenty of conscious thought and persistence, before the skill becomes habitual and effortless. Thinking skills can be learned in the same way. And we have to start by becoming conscious of our thought processes.

If I ask you to think about the town you grew up in, what happens in your mind? You might picture different familiar scenes, imagine the sounds, or even smells. That is, you will draw on all your internal senses, some more than others, either because you have stronger, clearer recollections, or are more at home with one sense than another. Perhaps you are happier with pictures than sounds, for example. Try it, and see for yourself what happens when you think.

Creating pictures in the mind

As well as remembering something from your own past, you

can also *create* a thought picture, perhaps when reading a graphic description of some far distant country you have never been to, or a piece of well-written fiction. To do this, you need to call on your store of countless millions of memories, as well as second-hand experiences from television, films, books and other descriptions. All these are reconstructed and intermixed to fit into an instant life-like mosaic of inner senses. You may have experienced being transported in your imagination when reading a good book. Radio drama can have a similar effect, as, unlike television, you are calling on more of your powers of imagination. A vivid imagination is as real as real life. After all, you use the same neurological pathways to represent internal experience as you do to represent external experience. Take a moment to imagine eating your favourite fruit. Not only will the electro-chemical charges in the brain be the same as when eating the fruit in reality, but so will your bodily reactions – you will actually feel yourself salivating.

Let us explore these thinking processes further. If I ask you to think about a fir tree, do you see a picture in your head? If you imagine walking through a pine wood, what is clearest – the sounds of the forest, birds, maybe wind in the trees, or the light shining through the branches, or maybe the feel of the fallen cones and brittle pieces of wood underfoot? Which of these senses comes to you most naturally? Would you find it easier to imagine a distant relative's voice, or to picture their face?

In doing these simple memory exercises you have been using your seeing, hearing and feeling senses subjectively, recalling and creating mental scenes as you wish. More importantly, you have been thinking about what is going on inside your mind. This is the first step to being able to control and use these processes for specific purposes.

In Western society the three primary senses are seeing, hearing and feeling. Although our senses of smell and taste can be very strong, and often unexpectedly bring to mind vivid memories, they constitute a very small part of our normal everyday thinking. They are therefore sometimes lumped together with feeling and touch when discussing internal senses. We use all three of these primary systems all the time although we may not be equally aware of them.

The sensory league table

Although the senses of the imagination mirror all five external senses, the term 'visualisation' is generally used to cover all of them. A lot of research has been carried out into how we visualise. One typical study showed that the most common mode of mental imaging was visual followed by hearing. Sensations of touch were less dominant, and those of taste and smell figured even less. The subjects were asked about their internal sensory impressions when imagining something. Their collated answers produced the following percentages:

visual	97
auditory	93
movement	74
touch	70
taste	67
smell	66
pain	54
temperature	43

This information tells us quite a lot. First, it is clear that all the senses can be 'imagined', although it is less common for some than others. So, if you have any difficulty in creating these sorts of thoughts – or inner senses – be confident that with a little practice you will be able to create them readily. Second, you will note that visual and auditory sensing – inwardly seeing and hearing – together account for most imagining. So the easiest way to improve your use of imagination is by first concentrating on seeing and hearing. With time and practice, other senses such as smell or taste, will become as easy to use as the more 'popular' ones.

The physical effects of thinking

Our bodies are directly affected by thought processes. Ask a small boy to imagine he is strong and brave, and watch him straighten up and push out his chest. Children can easily see themselves in another way, and the body simply takes on its new identity. Likewise for adults, if a restful, pleasant scene is visualised clearly, or a traumatic situation is imagined, the body responds accordingly. Real bodily responses are experienced, which, for better or worse, affect our health. We cannot separate thinking from behaviour. Each affects the other, but it is in the mind that behaviour is born.

Using your internal senses

Most people have some difficulty in creating and holding strong, clear, mental images of any kind. Our visualised thoughts are often transient and vague, and this may be partly because of the over-emphasis on rational, left-brain approaches in our Western education and professional training. Our adult lives are focused on outward circumstances and material things, rather than on inner reflection and meditation. But almost all of us used our imagination when we were children, in some cases having imaginary friends as real as real life. So it seems that our faculties for imagining have simply atrophied through non-use, and can easily be revived through practice and training. One mental skill at which we are all quite adept is that of worrying. Worried managers constantly imagine all sorts of corporate crises but they do not call on the visualisation skill of worrying – it calls on them. They do it, not by design, but by default. Imagine how our lives would improve if we could take control of all that mental energy and direct it into positive thought processes rather than negative ones.

How did you get on with the visualisation exercises at the beginning of this chapter? Three or four more tries might show a marked improvement, especially if you can get into a really relaxed state, and concentrate fully on re-living the past experience, or experiencing the imagined future scene or event. When using memory, go back as far as possible and see just how many of those stored-up memories you can access. Remember to switch from one sense to another – sights, sounds, feelings – to build up a complete panorama of the experience. When imagining something in the future, be ready to create the impossible, the bizarre – stretch your powers of imagination. Prove that you can take full control of your thoughts, and of yourself.

It is possible to have a thought in which all the senses are represented as originally recorded on the brain. But in the same way that you are not aware of all the senses externally (you may be very aware of the sunset, but not of the sound of gulls – or vice versa), you may have to recall each sense *separately* to be fully aware of them. In this way you can actually direct the way you think, and develop a better memory and a richer imagination.

Think of the first sights you saw during the few minutes after getting out of bed this morning. Separately, you should then be able to recall all the sounds during that period. And then the feelings – putting on your clothes, the feel of the toothbrush in your mouth, or the feel, smell and taste of hot tea or coffee. By recalling each sense separately and vividly, you will be able to understand, and then describe, what is happening more accurately. When experiencing vivid thoughts, you are lost to the world, even when wide awake. Have you ever missed meals when mentally absorbed in something, and found that time seemed to disappear? Pain is also considerably reduced (at the conscious level, which is all we need to be concerned about) when you are mentally absorbed.

At any given moment you will be processing external stimuli and also doing some of the internal sensing we call thinking, imagining or visualisation. Right now, you are not aware of your left foot . . . but now you are! Even when using your left foot for some important purpose, like walking or driving a car, you will still not be conscious of it – whatever remarkable tasks it is performing. As you are reading now, you might switch from a very conscious concentration on one or two words (using the verbal left brain) to a quick indulgence in an imagined picture that your mind throws up from some little association – possibly a long way from the immediate subject you are reading about. As well as converting the external stimuli – the words you see and read – you will conjure up a few pictures and feelings internally. As you read on and take in meaning, you are not *aware* of what is real or imagined, inside or outside – just the patterns of recognition and meaning that are constantly being etched on your consciousness.

Identifying your thinking preference

Although we use all our senses all the time, we do have preferences and tend to use one or two of them more than the others. This preference is usually established during childhood. Sometimes the internal use of a sense may simply reflect the way you have habitually used your senses in the outside world. An artist, for example, who is skilled at observing, will usually find it easy to visualise internally. A person who listens a lot, by preference or profession (and this includes most managers), will often be at home with inner sounds, particularly the spoken voice. This hearing ability is also very important for musicians. On the other hand, an architect would not succeed unless she or he was able to *see* the finished building.

35

So we each have preferences, or talents, for different ways of sensing. Here are some phrases that we all use from time to time which give excellent clues as to our individual preferences.

VISUAL

'She has a blind spot.'

'We don't see eye to eye.'

'It appears to me . . .'

'Show me . . .'

'Can you shed some light on this?'

'I've been looking closely at this.'

'It looks OK to me.'

AUDITORY

'That rings a bell.'

'It came across loud and clear.'

'He turned a deaf ear . . .'

'She described it word for word.'

'We're on the same wavelength.'

FEELING

'He's a cool customer.'

'I'll keep in touch.'

'Just hold on a minute.'

'We've hardly scratched the surface.'

'He got a warm response.'

Language is such an important part of our thinking that it is not surprising that we often express in words what is really going on inside us. Sometimes the words suggest very strongly, say, a visual way of thinking. What of the strange but common expression 'I can see what you are saying'? This expression only makes sense when we understand the different ways in which thoughts can be processed by different people. Words need not be visualised as words, but the language instantly produces in the mind a series of picture associations that make visual sense – to a visualising person.

Understanding the thinking style of others

An important aspect of management is the ability to work well with others and to do this we need to be able to recognise the thinking style of other members of the team. There are several kinds of clues to look out for.

Put your cards on the table

John Grinder and Richard Bindler, the pioneers of Neuro-Linguistic Programming (known as the science of personal excellence), conducted a simple but very interesting experiment with a therapy group. They took green, yellow and red cards, and had people go round to each member of the group and say why they were there. People who used a lot of words to do with feelings got a yellow card. Those who used a lot of words and phrases to do with hearing got green cards, and those who tended to use words to do with seeing got red cards.

Then there was a simple exercise. People with the same colour card had to sit down and talk to each other for five minutes. Then they sat down and talked to someone with a different coloured card. Profound differences were observed in rapport between the people. Not surprisingly, people with the same colour card got on much better.

Similarly revealing experiments have been done using the mirroring technique. In this case a person copies, or mirrors, the body language of their partner. If the partner leans forward, the other party will do the same, matching the speed and tone of the voice as well as the general body posture. Because our total physiology reflects the way we think, mirroring produces the same inter-personal harmony as in the coloured cards experiment. People do feel happier with those who think and act like them – unless, that is, the person starts mimicking their stutter or twitch!

The eyes have it

We can also identify a person's preferred thinking system by the way their eyes move. These movements are known as 'eye accessing cues'.

Let me demonstrate. What is the first thing you see when you walk through the door of your office? To be able to answer this question you probably looked slightly up and to your left. That is how most right-handed people remember images.

If I then ask you how it feels to stroke a cat, you will probably look down and to your right, which is the way most people access feelings. At least this is what you would have

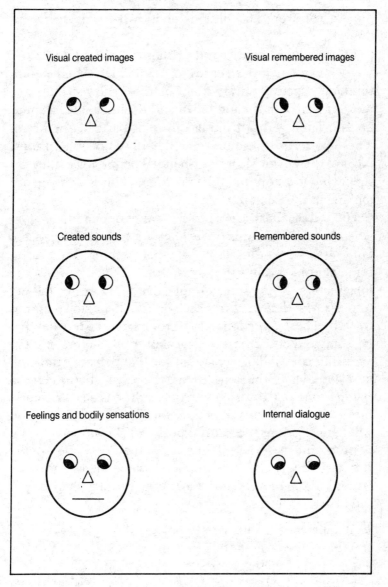

Pattern of eye movements

done if you were not thinking about what your eyes were doing!

This eye movement is quite systematic and relates to the way we use our inner senses, or modalities, when we are thinking. Neurological studies have shown that eye movements, both up and down and to either side, seem to be associated with activating different parts of the brain. These patterns of eye movement apply to people in most parts of the world. Most right-handed people's eyes move in the ways shown on the previous page. (This is as if you are looking at the person.)

You will see that the eye position varies depending first on whether sights, sounds or feelings are being experienced, but also depending on whether senses are being remembered from the past, or 'created' with the imagination. Notice, for example, that when we are 'talking to ourselves' the eye direction will usually be down and to the left. These directions *may* be reversed for a left-handed person, as between right and left. But a person's eye accessing cues will be consistent for that person – they will always tend to be the same, even if they do not fit the general pattern of the pictures above. Although you can consciously move your eyes in any direction you like, unconsciously you will tend to adopt the natural positions shown here.

By asking a series of questions requiring use of the different internal representations, you can establish the pattern of eye movements. To activate visual memories you might ask:

- What colour is your front door?
- What is the largest book in your house?
- Can you visualise the first car you ever had?

To activate created representations, not based on memory, you might ask:

- What would your desk look like if it were painted turquoise?
- What would a double-decker Jaguar car look like?

And so on, for remembered and created sounds, feelings, and inner dialogue.

Remember that it is the *thought process* that dictates the internal use of the senses, and this might not exactly reflect spoken answers. So spoken answers can be ignored – just watch the eyes. Also, a question that *seems* to require visualisation might be treated differently by the person – for example you might internally *feel* the sides on a fifty pence coin rather than visualise it. An apparently inconsistent eye cue might be easily explained if the person is asked afterwards to describe whether they thought of a picture, sound, or a shape or texture.

Sometimes a question produces a very quick eye movement which is hard to spot. In other cases it might take time – for instance if a person is asked about the largest book in their house, they may need to do a mental tour of more than one room. In this case they might handle as well as look at the books, in which case there would be a whole range of internal sensory impressions, with corresponding eye movements.

Other clues to thinking style

There are a number of other clues as to what is going on in our thought processes. A person thinking in a visual mode will generally speak quickly and at a higher pitch. Pictures happen so fast that you need to talk fast to keep up with them. Auditory thinkers, will, on the other hand, probably speak with a clear tone of voice, shoulders at an angle, just as when listening to something, and small rhythmic movements in the body might be noticed. Internal dialogue is sometimes seen in the slight movement of the lips as the person verbalises. Thinking back to the coloured card experiment, you can now begin to see the importance of using the same representational system when you communicate with others.

For example, a conversation between a visualiser and a feeling person can be very frustrating. The visual thinker will be impatiently tapping his foot, and the feeling person will not understand what all the rush is about.

Clearly, it is useful to be aware of the preferred thinking style of business colleagues, family and friends. You can then start to increase your rapport by matching their thinking style. Managers will find this technique invaluable in improving their relationships with their staff. Furthermore, there are obvious advantages for anyone whose job involves selling. For example, in selling a car to a feeling person, you might not get very far talking at length about the many features of the new model, and similarly you might be wasting your time showing brochures and admiring the car's visual lines from different angles. But sit the person in the driver's seat, let him or her *feel* the well-upholstered seat, the sporty steering wheel, and the smooth gear changes – and you are sure to make a sale.

Do not worry if these various methods of identifying other people's thinking style seem difficult to put into practice at first. Once you become aware of the importance of linguistic clues, eye movements, posture and tone of voice, you will find yourself noticing them all the time in the course of casual, everyday conversation with clients and colleagues. Taken together, these clues will give you an instinctive and invaluable knowledge of other people's thinking preferences.

Understanding your own thinking style

If you think back to the memory exercises earlier, what was the first sense that captured the memory, and from which you re-lived the experience? Was it a sight, a sound or a feeling? You probably do not remember. But if you try this again, and one or two different memory exercises, you might spot a recurring preference – the sense that initially brings recall. This is known as your 'lead system'. Interestingly, it need not be the same as your primary system – the sense preference you have when handling conscious experience and thought in the present. And it may vary with different kinds of thought. For instance, you may use pictures to get in touch with painful experiences, and sounds to recall pleasant ones. Try some more remembering and imagining exercises along the lines of those you have already done, but this time note especially your lead system.

If an unconscious lead system is generating painful feelings and images, a person will feel bad without knowing why. You can imagine the benefits, therefore, of not just knowing what your preferred representation system is, but also of being able to easily access and describe your thought processes. More than anything else, this will give you an understanding of yourself – which is the foundation of any self-improvement. These benefits are then multiplied, particularly in a management job, if you are also able to understand and allow for the thinking preferences of others.

Your personal synesthesia

The ability to switch from one sense to another when thinking is known as 'synesthesia'. For instance sounds might conjure up visual memories, or abstract imagery, or colours – which in turn you might link to moods. This ability to switch at will between the inner senses is usually a feature of those with a particularly good memory, or perhaps those who are gifted artistically. We sometimes talk of tonal colour in music, loud colours and warm sounds. In painting, colours are classified from cold blues to warm reds. This ability to switch senses is quite common, and seems to be wired into us from birth, though people have great difficulty in understanding why certain senses bring associations with others. Nevertheless it has been shown that a person's blood pressure and pulse rate will increase in a red environment, and drop if the surroundings are mostly blue. And people actually experience the feel of coolness in a blue room – even if the temperature is above normal!

Personal synesthesia happens automatically – but we can also develop this skill. A pleasant memory can usually be guided from one sensation to another. Having captured the visual scene, it is then easier to recall the sounds, and then more subtle feelings and sensations. Exploring a memory in this way you will create a very strong overall association which will make recall progressively easier, as you mentally practise the exercise.

Why not try it? Think back to some pleasant experience. This time go back further in time – perhaps to your early childhood. As you dwell on the experience and savour in turn all the sights, sounds and feelings, you will recapture the surrounding feeling of well-being, joy or security – your emotional state at the time – as well as the separate recollections of each inner sense. On returning to the present, objective world you can then face any situation in a more positive, resourceful state of mind.

The submodalities of your inner senses

So far we have only addressed the main senses of seeing, hearing and feeling in general terms. But now we can take this understanding a lot further.

Consider, for example, a visual memory. Look at it in detail. Is the picture big or small, clear or blurred, in colour or black and white? And are you seeing the memory as if through your own eyes, or as an observer looking from the outside? Is there movement, or do you see a series of still pictures? Similar questions can be applied to each main 'modality' or representational system – seeing, hearing and feeling. There are many ways to describe these differences, termed 'submodalities', and some of the common ones are listed as examples.

SEEING

Is it a movie or a still photograph?

Is the image bright, dim or dark?

How close is the image to you?

Are you in the picture or watching from a distance?

Is it three-dimensional, or two-dimensional?

Is there any part you particularly focus on?

Is the image on the right, left or in the centre?

Is there anything about the image that triggers strong feelings?

HEARING

Are you saying something to yourself, or hearing it from others?

How loud, fast, and in what sort of tone?

Where is the sound coming from?

Are there words or other sounds?

How far are you from the sound?

Is it continuous or discontinuous?

Is there anything special about the sound?

Does anything else trigger strong emotions?

FEELING

What is the temperature – hot or cold?

Are the feelings steady or intermittent?

Is the texture rough or smooth?

Is there any pressure? Where is it located?

Is the weight heavy or light?

Does anything else trigger strong emotions?

Some of these questions may not apply, but it is useful to have a checklist to help explore and describe your inner sensations in as much detail as possible. With practice it will become easier to be aware of these many submodalities. Do not be disappointed if you have difficulty at first, or if the process seems like nonsense. There is a whole world of imagery inside you and a journey into this world can be as surprising and exciting as any science fiction space exploration. The difference is that this is *your reality*. You can create your own inner universe which will be reflected in all your actions and achievements. A little patience in getting to know your inner self will pay generous dividends.

Changing your reality

All these submodalities have a profound effect on how you feel – together, they *are* your feelings. By accessing happy, productive memories, and describing the submodalities, you will begin to recognise which submodalities are associated with pain and which with pleasure; which are productive and which are unproductive; which will help you change behaviour and get the results you desire. You can then recall an unpleasant memory, and, by changing the submodalities one by one, actually change the way you feel about the experience.

Let us take a specific example. Most managers put public speaking at the top of their 'fear' list. How would you use your new understanding of submodalities to change the way you feel about giving presentations and speeches? First recall a painful past experience, perhaps when you were very embarrassed and you had made a real mess of a presentation. Then think of an occasion when everything went right – it might have been another speech or presentation but it could have been a different activity. Compare the submodalities of each experience – they will differ, which is why the two experiences produce very different feelings when recalled. Use the checklist to explore your memory fully.

Now identify the various features of the pleasant experience, and apply them to the unpleasant one. If, in the pleasant case, you could see everything as through your own eyes in bright colours, then make these changes to the other memory. It is the balance between the various senses and their submodalities that determines how you feel about anything. And you can change it all. You might, for instance, want to make your bad memories distant, dark and out of focus. If you wish, you can make voices quite different. Do you ever have a voice inside that nags or criticises you? Try slowing it down, speeding it up, changing the tone, making it quieter then louder. Observe the effects these changes have.

Many painful, negative associations are concerned with people and relationships. Perhaps you have a particular business colleague – whether a boss, peer or subordinate – who always seems to 'get under your skin' or 'bring out the worst in you', leaving you feeling belittled, irritated or just plain angry. Alternatively, the person might be a client or customer, in which case more sensitivity may be demanded, thus further exacerbating the poor relationship and 'painful' association. Most managers have experienced such relationship problems. Using your newfound ability to control your own submodalities, you can remove these deep-rooted aversions to people or activities. First of all, explore as much as possible each submodality of the pleasurable event or relationship. Go back through the checklist – was the image large or small, clear or blurred, associated (as if seen through your eyes) or dissociated (as if seen through someone else's eyes, with you in the picture)? What about the sounds? What other feelings could you recall about the positive, pleasant memory? Then, one by one, swap the submodalities of the unpleasant experience with those of the pleasant one. Repeated visualisation of the painful experience with all its submodalities exchanged for positive ones will enable you to change the way you feel when the real event or personal contact occurs. This is because of the new *association* you have created in your mind – which is where the (probably quite irrational) negative feelings originated in the first place, and were reinforced through constant repetition.

These are simple DIY techniques which can be applied in whatever ways you choose. Make your own list of tasks, events, relationships, responsibilities and situations which you find distasteful, painful or negative in any way. These are your applications. Now list a few pleasant experiences which will provide you with the mental raw material to make the changes. Just be confident that you can change any part of any mental recording, however habitual its associations have become. You can turn a mental screen from black and white to colour and back again at will. Try it. You can zoom in and zoom out. You can change your boss's voice to that of a three-year-old child. In short, you are the master of your own mind, and so of your feelings and behaviour. You just need plenty of clear, positive visualisation to overwhelm existing negative patterns and associations. This has an immediate and dramatic effect on behaviour and personal achievement. It can change a mediocre manager into an outstanding leader; a failure-type personality into a success.

You are now beginning to use some of that unknown, inaccessible part of your mind. The silent right brain is being called on to display its wondrous powers of imagination, leaving language and logic on the sidelines and enormously enhancing your creativity and efficiency as a manager. In the next chapter we refine these thinking skills even further.

4

CHANGING YOUR VIEWPOINT

S EEING COMES AT THE TOP of the sensual popularity
ratings. When describing what happens when we think,
mental pictures – images – are found to account for much of
the process. And we have already seen that this is a particular feature of right-brain thinking.

But there are other ways in which we 'see'. The interpretation of what we see – the meaning we give it – is unique
to each of us; our *perception* is different. We also speak of
seeing things from a different perspective, seeing, in effect,
from somebody else's viewpoint. We ask ourselves what someone
else would think, feel or do, in order to shed new light on a
problem. More specifically, we try *not* to see in our own
habitual, patterned way, looking for any other perspective
that might bring further understanding. This is sometimes
referred to as 'reframing'.

So we see with our eyes, with our brains, and as if through
somebody else's eyes and brain – from a different perspective. Each of these ways of seeing affects the way we behave,
so better 'seeing' will mean more successful, purposeful
behaviour. And such behaviour will quickly enable us to
achieve our personal and professional goals.

What you see with your eyes

You may think you can 'believe it if you see it' but what you actually see with your eyes is far from a 'true' image of the world. Amazingly, your eyes take in less than a trillionth of the electro-magnetic energy that reaches them. So you simply cannot experience the world as it really is – you automatically exclude almost all of it before it even reaches your nervous system.

Some experiments with frogs illustrate the way in which eyes filter out irrelevant visual information. Jerry Lettvin, at Massachusetts Institute of Technology, devised an experiment in which an immobilised frog was placed at the centre of a hemisphere seven inches in radius. Small objects could be placed in different positions on the inner surface of this hemisphere or moved around in the space inside it. Then micro-electrodes were implanted in the frog's optic nerve to measure, as the title of the classic paper expressed it, 'What the frog's eye tells the frog's brain'.

Out of the infinite number of different visual patterns presented to the frog -- colours, shapes, movements, and combinations of these – the researchers found that only four kinds of 'messages' were actually sent from the retina to the brain. These four types of visual stimuli were all important for the frog's survival. For instance the brain would be informed of any significant movement, or of a sudden decrease in the amount of light, as it would when a large enemy was attacking. Likewise, any small dark objects coming into the field of vision and moving close to the eye were likely to be flying insects, identified as the next meal, and therefore readily perceived as vital for survival.

Whilst we humans are certainly not as blinkered as frogs, this experiment offers some interesting parallels with the narrow perceptive mechanisms which allow us to cope in our own environment. Although our eyes function with amazing sophistication, they are highly specialised and selective, handling only a tiny proportion of the countless potential messages from the outside world.

Many experiments have shown that, contrary to popular belief, sight does not take place in the eyes, but *with the assistance of the eyes*. The first part of the process is what the eye tells the brain; the second part is what the brain tells the eye.

Until our brains make sense of the visual information selected by our eyes there is no understanding, no consciousness, no 'reality'. To you and me, reality begins when we see with the brain, and make personal meaning out of the colourless, formless mystery of the so-called material world.

Your brain's filing system

How then does your brain make sense of the data your eyes provide, however limited the input?

The brain amasses its information in much the same way as you use a filing system. Information is brought together and classified subject by subject. As far as possible, everything has a home, and can be accessed easily later. As with any filing system, there is a hierarchy of subject matter: 'Susan' is a file which includes Susan's school report and Susan's toothache, and anything about Susan. She belongs in a filing drawer called 'family'. She also appears in another one called 'scholar', another called 'female', and another called 'girls' names beginning with S'. You can imagine, then, that there is a lot of cross-referencing. Toothache, for example, appears in another drawer called, perhaps, 'aches and pains', as well as one called 'dentistry'. The cross-referencing is comprehensive and almost instantaneous, so that you can immediately make sense of 'Susan's toothache' in the context of other things about Susan and anyone else's toothache.

Although your brain files information away phenomenally quickly, and can recall it just as quickly when needed, the information is often very incomplete. This is partly because of the limited data taken in by our eyes, but also because the unobliging world just happens to be like that – we do not always see all there is to be seen about an event or situation.

Take a chair, for instance, a concept that has a place in almost everyone's mental filing system. The chair might only have two legs, but your brain can quickly fill in the missing information and classify it as a chair. Alternatively it will find a home somewhere in the right cabinet drawer as 'a broken chair'. If seen as 'bits of broken furniture' or 'wooden sticks', classification will be equally fast and efficient.

This classification process allows you to make sense of otherwise unmanageable volumes of data, and happens quickly enough for you to cope in your everyday world. You meet an acquaintance from a number of years ago, for example. There is immediate recognition – the person has been instantly associated with some part of your filing system, however long ago you last saw them, and however much they have changed in appearance. After a couple of minutes a name might be put to the face, and soon you will recall all the related information you need to make full sense of that 'seeing' experience. All this happens so unconsciously that you take it for granted, and is so sophisticated an operation that a filing cabinet, or even a computerised database, is a poor analogy.

This tendency to classify everything, and make meaningful 'patterns', has weaknesses as well as strengths. Edward de Bono (of lateral thinking fame) used a different analogy. He described the brain as a landscape, a tract of barren land, on which rain – the stimuli of the five senses – falls to form streams and rivulets, and in time swelling rivers and deep gorges. As the rain continues to fall, its final resting place is determined not by where the drops fall, but by the shape of the landscape that has already been formed by earlier rainfall, and earlier, less marked contours. In time, river courses become fixed, and a consistent pattern is etched on the landscape, into which the rainfall is channelled. In the same way, as classifications or patterns become ever more embedded on the landscape of your brain, new sensory stimuli are habitually and conveniently channelled into old, familiar watercourses. New meanings and insights are sacrificed for efficiency and convenience.

The power of mental habits

Much so-called creative or lateral thinking is concerned with breaking out of this habitual mode of thinking, accepting messages through the senses as if on a pristine landscape, untouched by past experience and not constrained by any kind of classification. Such a holistic view is the main feature of right-brain thinking. It is the rationalising, pattern-making tendency that belongs with the left brain, and this often dominates the thinking of managers and professionally trained people.

A simple exercise will help illustrate this. Look at the two simple drawings on the next page and decide which vertical line is longer – A or B.

Even if you have seen this sort of optical exercise before, you will no doubt say that A appears to be longer than B. In fact B is slightly longer than A, if you measure it accurately!

Why does the vertical line on the left appear longer than the one on the right, when the reverse is true? Maybe you

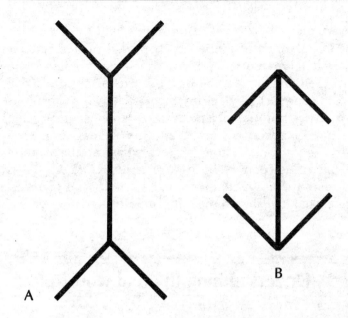

picture the left-hand one as the far corner of a room or the inside of a box, and assume that with the effect of distance and perspective it will look smaller, and your mental landscape of known thought patterns (quite wrongly) makes due allowance. Conversely, the right-hand line is perhaps seen to be the front corner of a building or cube, so no allowance is made for distance. Either way, what you see is not what you actually see (a simple line drawing), but some existing perception in your mind that is quickly superimposed on the image.

In order to function normally you have to assume a lot about the world you perceive. If I tell you that Bob is in a room, you immediately assume that the room has four walls, a floor, a ceiling, and probably furniture. On entering the room you don't expect to have to check whether the walls are perpendicular and at right angles to each other. If you constantly had to inspect everything in your environment, you would have no time to do anything.

So we make all sorts of assumptions, and this results in some mistakes. For example, if a special, distorted room is created that is narrower and has a much lower ceiling at the far end, on seeing a person walk towards that end you will think they are actually getting bigger. However ridiculous this is, the assumption of a rectilinear room is so strong that your mind is totally confused, and may believe an impossibility (the person getting bigger), whilst not believing a possibility (the room being smaller at one end). All this is because of the brain's tendency to create efficient patterns, to give what it *thinks* is a meaningful interpretation.

Understanding the real world

We each consider our own personal world to be reality. Time after time, we make the mistake of assuming that our personal world is *the* world – the objective, real world.

Thankfully, because our eyes and brains have the same basic structure, we form broadly similar patterns through a common education and culture, and can live together in relative harmony.

But this is where you and I, despite our restricted vision, can outsmart the frog. As you read and think and imagine, you can begin to be aware of these mysteries of the thinking process, through a patently higher level of consciousness, and grasp the unlimited capacity of your brain. You can effortlessly comprehend a frog's tunnel vision, famine in Africa, discounted cash flow, or black holes. Moreover, you can change your perceptions as you desire, you can think whatever you decide to think, you can believe whatever you decide to believe – the only limit is your imagination. Human experience is just the result of 'incubated imaginings' – thoughts turn into reality after a time. And because the only true reality is our individual, inner reality, we can change *our world* – the only real world there is – and create our own future.

Although we inhabit a somewhat different environment to that of the frog, our perceptions also tend to respond to our own environment in a survival-type way. The pygmies of the Congo have their own special environment. Dwelling mainly in dense forest, they rarely see long distances, so they have not developed a strong sense of size and distance as we have. Colin Turnbull, an anthropologist who studied pygmies, once took his pygmy guide on a tour outside the forest. As they were crossing a wide plain, they saw a herd of buffalo in the distance. Turnbull's account of what followed is a remarkable illustration of how our perceptions are subject to conditioning by our particular environment:

> *Kenge looked over the plain and down to a herd of buffalo some miles away. He asked me what kind of insects they were, and I told him buffalo, twice as big as the forest buffalo known to him. He laughed loudly and told me not to tell him such stupid stories. . . We got into the car and drove down to where the animals were grazing. He watched them getting larger and larger, and though he was as courageous as any pygmy, he moved over and sat close to me and muttered that it was witchcraft. . . When he realised they were real buffalo he was no longer afraid, but what puzzled him was why they had been so small, and whether they had really been small and suddenly grown larger or whether it had been some kind of trickery.*

Unfamiliar sights seemed to play tricks on Kenge's mind. The buffalo did not fit into his pygmy patterns.

Seeing things from a different angle

Whilst there is not much you can do about the limitations of the human optical process, nor is it always easy to overcome long-standing patterns of thinking, you *can* start trying to see things from another perspective. 'Reframing', or seeing things from a different viewpoint, can change just about any situation you face as a manager.

For instance, there is the story of the man who woke up with a rusty spring from his mattress sticking into his back. This gave him the idea for a stylish egg cup which he then successfully marketed, making a fortune. It doesn't matter whether or not the story is true. It simply illustrates how reframing an event or situation can make all the difference. What at first glance seems to be a problem, can turn out to be a golden opportunity. A shower of rain might be a godsend for a farmer but play havoc with the village fête. By changing the frame, you change the meaning, and correspondingly how you feel and behave.

The idea of seeing things from a different angle is one we meet constantly. The punch line of a good joke often surprises you by the way the meaning is turned round, and another angle is seen. It is all to do with upsetting existing mental patterns. You need to place events and circumstances in some frame or other to give them meaning. Depending on the meaning you assign to anything, you will feel differently about it. By mentally changing perspective, your behaviour and feelings can change dramatically. The way you see circumstances will not only change your behaviour and feelings, but can affect your future – which is determined by your present.

Why not list half a dozen 'broken springs' that bother you as a manager – things you could well do without and instinctively try to eliminate, delegate, or just painfully endure? Now try and create an 'egg cup' from each – a creative solution that will bring you some benefit. See the problem in a different light. What about the nuisance of being constantly interrupted by staff so that your time is not your own? Your office door never seems to be closed for five minutes. There are situations, of course, in which it is right to be interrupted, and it is important to be seen as open and available to your staff when needed. So why not have an open door policy and also a closed door policy – say an open door on each afternoon except Friday (when you want time to clear outstanding tasks), and a closed door policy in the mornings (or whichever way suits you) when you are not to be interrupted on matters that can wait a couple of hours. This sort of reframe will not only solve your problem, it is also likely to improve your overall effectiveness and control of time. And you will probably get more respect from your staff for recognising them, whilst not neglecting your role as a manager.

To see an apparent problem from another, or preferably several angles, brings all sorts of tangible benefits at no cost. And this requires the use of right-brain powers, particularly imagination. Reframing is not just about seeing the world through rose-tinted spectacles, pretending everything is better than it really is. It is not just positive thinking and making positive statements to yourself. Problems may not vanish when you see them in another light (although sometimes they do), but the more ways you have of seeing them the more chances there are of finding a solution. It is always better to have an option, and better still to have several. Having extra perspectives can improve the way you do what you already do.

Inter-personal reframing

Most of the problems you face as a manager will probably, directly or indirectly, concern communication – between people, functions and departments. For this reason, a great

deal of management training is concerned with inter-
personal and presentation skills, but often with too much
emphasis on external behaviour rather than thoughts, attitudes, and the purpose of communication. Being able to see
things from the other person's viewpoint is not just an
indispensable first step to better communication, it can
often eliminate the problem altogether, and the wasted time
and effort associated with it. Or, better still, it can help
generate new win–win situations when everyone comes out
better off. The essence of good communication is to understand and take account of the other person's needs, to see
things from their perspective.

In any form of negotiation or selling, if you understand
the other person's motives, you can avoid conceding on
issues that need no concession. At the same time you can
stress matters that are of importance to the other party,
however unimportant they may be to you, and thus finish
with a better deal – for both sides. No clever mental techniques are needed in this case, just a bit of imagination.
Simply ask yourself: 'How would I feel? How would I react
in his or her position?' The right questions bring the right
answers, and this type of empathy is a natural ability we all
have. Although sometimes a little rusty, it just needs to be
practised and developed.

Context reframing

There are two main forms of reframing. The first is just to
see things in a different context, or setting. Telling a pack of
lies to your boss might truncate a promising career, but the
imaginative use of pure fiction – the literary version of the
same thing – has earned many novelists a fortune. Indeci-
sion can be a costly negative characteristic for a manager,
but might be a welcome trait when wondering whether to
tender your resignation after a single emotional confronta-
tion. By identifying a context in which the negative or

counterproductive behaviour is seen to be positive, the behaviour can be viewed more positively and objectively.

Let us say a manager is in the habit of not maintaining eye contact when speaking one to one, or addressing a small group. This all-too-common trait can quickly erode the listener's attention and respect. In some cultures, however, it is a mark of disrespect to make eye contact when addressing a person of a certain social standing. Etiquette demands that the eyes are lowered. So the behaviour, in this new context, is actually praiseworthy. In other words, it is sometimes acceptable and at other times unacceptable, depending on the context. Recognising this objectively, the manager will change the behaviour because it is a mark of respect in our Western society and is known to improve the effectiveness of communication. It is no longer an issue, just something that needs to be changed, for specific reasons.

Context reframing usually helps when people say things like: 'I wish I could stop doing. . .' or 'I'm too. . . .' In what situations would such behaviour be acceptable, or even admirable? If you visualise the new, more acceptable context, then imagine a different, more fitting behaviour in the original context, making the change will be not be a painful internal battle, but a sensible compromise negotiated in a positive way.

Let us say you find it difficult to make your feelings known in company meetings, frequently wishing, after the event, that you had been more effective in getting across your point of view. In some situations this would be quite acceptable – perhaps if you were the most junior person attending, or were unfamiliar with the subject under discussion, or there was plenty of time for reflection before any decision had to be made. In these and other contexts your behaviour would be acceptable or even laudable. However, depending on your role in a meeting, it might be better to be ready to speak out strongly before the opportunity is lost. From this perspective, changing your behaviour is no longer such a big issue – because it is kept to its context. Having seen things objectively, and without berating yourself for being timid or tongue-tied, you can make full preparation for your next meeting, mentally rehearsing what you intend to say.

Content reframing

The other approach is to reframe the content of a situation or some aspect of behaviour. This involves focusing on whatever you want, to give the meaning you want to give. Advertisers do it all the time, when they direct attention to some aspect of a product or service. Politicians do the same. They can make economic figures mean whatever they want them to mean, by breaking them down, redefining the content, or presenting them differently to show a different picture. To reframe content, you need to ask: 'What else could this mean?' or 'How else could I describe this behaviour?'

As a plant manager, let us say you are running 15 per cent down on your available capacity. This sounds bad. You can present it, however, as running at 85 per cent efficiency – which sounds pretty good. Or you might show that you have reduced your order backlog more than in the previous six months (which actually wasn't difficult but still sounds good). Choosing the content reframe, you might show that one of your competitors, or a similar industry, lagged well behind your performance, or that you had managed to maintain high staff morale, or that you had carefully built in machine maintenance time as a positive, long-term productivity measure. No single perspective is right. Each throws a little more light on a situation, and gives you a deeper understanding.

Other reframing techniques

Another technique is to aim to generate an agreed quota of alternatives. Put a number on it – say ten. The number should not be so large as to render the exercise impossible, nor so small as not to harness your enormous creative potential. The advantage of a quota or target number of options or ideas is that you carry on generating new ideas, rather than accepting the first, perhaps most obvious one. It also means you have to *do* something specific, and this will help you make the transition from the logical approach you may be used to.

Old-fashioned brainstorming, which goes back to the fifties, is still effective in generating ideas in groups. Other newer techniques are being used in some of the largest corporations. One so-called 'provocation technique' uses what are termed 'reversal statements'. Statements about a company's market or products, such as 'We make tools that last a lifetime', are *reversed* to become, for example, 'We make tools that last a short time'. This sort of reframe, or provocation, might produce, for example, ideas for throw-away tools, as has been the case with razors, cheap pens and plastic cups. Or the reverse statement might be, 'We make non-tools', which might suggest other markets using similar technology but outside the traditional tools field – perhaps ornaments or toys. At Du Pont, they used this technique to search for new applications for a Lycra fibre. Reversing their past thinking, which was confined to garments (applications for people), they searched for applications for 'non-people'. As a result, new ideas and Lycra products are being generated.

Another simple but fascinating technique that has proved effective in business is known as 'metaphor thinking'. In this case, ideas are generated by linking the problem with something in a totally unrelated field, such as the world of nature. Again, at Du Pont, for example, they had to develop a fire-

63

resistant Nomex aramid fibre that could be dyed without requiring special procedures in customers' mills. The material's tight fibre structure baffled researchers until one asked what made it possible to enter a coal mine. The answer: props that keep the tunnel from collapsing. Applying the mining metaphor, they were able to change the molecular structure of the Nomex which then allowed dyes to enter whilst the fibres were 'propped up'. As a result, a dyeable, flame-resistant Nomex is being used for aircraft interiors in a variety of colours.

What all these techniques have in common is the use of right-brain modes of thinking – the ability to visualise mentally, relating otherwise unimportant information by association, and reframing.

The advantages of reframing

The term 'lateral thinking', coined by Edward de Bono back in the sixties, also refers to finding better ways of looking at things. Lateral, or sideways, again suggests a creative, non-linear way of thinking, the mode of the right brain, rather than the logical, sequential pattern of the left brain.

Thinking laterally and reframing are natural processes. The mind is quite capable of seeing things from different perspectives, or in a different context. However, by placing such undue emphasis on our skills, we have severely reduced our ability to think laterally. In left-brain problem solving, we tend to employ different kinds of methods: 'Get the facts, write down the pros and cons, evaluate the options, do a strengths, weaknesses, opportunities, threats analysis'. We are thus calling on the linguistic left hemisphere to address the problem, one logical step at a time. But alternative techniques are needed if we are to call on the resources of the right brain, to think laterally, to see differently.

In left-brain mode, or what has by default become our 'natural' mode, the search stops when we reach a promising solution. Thinking has served its purpose. It was a means to an end, and we now carry on with the important managerial task of applying the thinking or implementing the solution. In a lateral search, however, the mental work goes on, finding one possible solution after another – without evaluating or finalising any of them, however initially plausible they may seem. The left-brain search throws out unreasonable ideas – it cannot cope with unreasonableness. But the lateral right brain does not classify them. After all, seen in a different context, or when reframed, an apparently ludicrous idea might turn out to be the best solution, or at least a starting point for a new line of questioning.

Questioning is itself a way to break down established mind patterns. Creative people tend to ask better questions, and get better answers. With a big enough 'why', you will often come up with the 'how' you are looking for.

Although creative thought is mainly associated with spontaneous flashes of intuition, the lateral search can be a deliberate one; somehow we have to stimulate that part of our thinking. It does not mean that the first, most obvious solution is not accepted, just that its adoption is delayed. And when adopted, the obvious solution will not be chosen because it is the only one, but because it is the *best* of several – and this tends to improve the quality of the decision. No choice is Hobson's choice. Two alternatives might present a dilemma. Three or more will give you more freedom and control. In any event, the habit and practice of looking for several alternative approaches, and the thinking skills acquired, will benefit you in the future.

So thinking involves seeing, in both a physical and perceptual sense. What you think you see is determined by the way you interpret things according to your store of concepts and meanings, values and beliefs – your unique brain patterns. It is your brain that really does the seeing. And by using your right brain more fully another world of seeing will open up, another world of possibility and achievement.

5

A BETTER STATE OF MIND

THE WAY YOU SEE THINGS can make you feel happy or sad,
good or bad. And learning to see things in a different
way can change your whole attitude to life. When you are in
a successful state of mind, you tend to succeed. When you
feel creative, you are sure to accomplish more. Better thinking results in a better state of mind, and vice versa.

All your inner perceptions of sights, sounds and feelings
add up to produce this overall state of mind. Indeed, it is the
specific submodalities of the sounds, images and feelings
going on inside, rather than the subject matter of your
thoughts, that produce the happiness or sadness you associate with that particular experience. You might have two
unpleasant memories of entirely different events, but they
produce a similar state of mind because of the mixture of
submodalities you experienced. Conversely, you might recall memories with very similar content – different sales
interviews, different flights to Paris, monthly staff meetings
– and each, having different submodalities, might arouse
very different feelings. One might produce pleasure, the
other pain.

Everything you do is related to the pleasure or pain you
associate with that behaviour. You do what you do either

because you expect to gain pleasure, or avoid pain, or both. Note that your actions are based on what you *believe* will give you pleasure or pain, and this belief is based on the perceptions of your experience to date, the associations you have built into mental patterns – your conditioning.

So, to get a rough, subjective measure of your psychological or emotional state, you could place your feelings somewhere on the scale between extreme pain and great pleasure.

Pain_____**Pleasure**

Setting goals

Goal-setting has long been recognised as a major factor in personal and management success. Knowing what you want to achieve is a prerequisite of any change in behaviour.

But what are the characteristics of the goals we set ourselves? First, they usually involve a state of mind, as well as some outward or material achievement. For example, you may be aiming to achieve 'financial security'. This is very hard to define in absolute terms, and its precise meaning will vary from person to person. But it is above all a state of mind – the feeling that you will not be at the mercy of financial ups and downs, the peace of mind that you associate with not having to rely on others to maintain what you see as an acceptable standard of living. The pleasure you link with financial security – the state of mind – is the goal you are really striving after, whether consciously or unconsciously.

Interim goals

Pleasure may be our ultimate goal but most people also have interim goals – stepping stones to longer-term, larger-scale, perhaps less tangible desires. For instance, you may want to attain further professional or other qualifications or a better job, not for their own sake, but in order to gain financial security, respect, power or popularity. In the same way, a desire to lose weight is likely to be a stepping stone on the way to a generally healthier lifestyle. Because each interim goal is just one step on the way to somewhere else, achieving any single goal rarely brings with it a lasting sense of satisfaction.

Your personal hierarchy of goals

All these interim goals are staging posts in the search for something more fundamental – the pleasure, happiness and self-fulfilment that you and I as humans strive towards. Your interim goals will thus form a hierarchy leading to your ultimate goal, which is so intangible a concept, so much a state of mind, that you will probably have difficulty defining it.

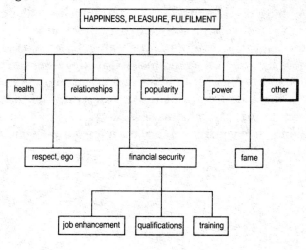

It might be helpful for you to draw up your own hierarchy of goals. Some of those on the chart shown may not apply in your case, and others not referred to might occur to you. Each interim goal can be broken down into as much detail as you wish. For instance, the 'qualifications' stepping stone would need to detail below it the specific qualifications you want, and smaller goals about how to get accepted for courses, how to find the money to pay for them, or how to find the time you will need for study. The health goal will also no doubt have subsidiary objectives concerning exercise and diet.

This personal goals exercise will not just make things clearer in your own mind, it will also highlight any goals that are in conflict. The long hours working towards that promotion might not be consistent with your resolution to take more exercise or to put more time into relationships you consider important. It is better to spot the conflicts *before* they start causing problems in your life.

The ultimate goal, however, is a state of mind – call it pleasure, happiness or whatever you wish. And because a state of mind can be created – by changing the characteristics of your thoughts – the ultimate goal is achievable. You can decide what you want to feel. And you might find you no longer have to strive for some of your interim goals because you have discovered a way to bypass them and go straight for the happiness you're really seeking.

As we have seen, we tend to associate different situations, events and tasks with how we feel about them – whether they bring pleasure or pain. And how we feel inevitably affects our actual performance. But our state of mind can be changed. We just need to learn a few simple techniques.

Reaching the right state of mind

Much research has been done on the distinctive wave patterns of the brain, both during sleep and in various states of consciousness. The brain wavelengths associated with a restful, relaxed, yet receptive frame of mind are known as alpha waves, a relatively low frequency of between eight and fourteen cycles per second, or hertz (Hz). It is at these levels that we are most open to the subconscious creative insights and imagery associated with the right-brain hemisphere.

Too much conscious thought, predominantly using the left brain operating at higher wave frequencies, can be accompanied by stress, with all its harmful effects. But to be in a relaxed, alert and receptive physical and mental state is positively beneficial – in all kinds of ways. It is in this state that the creative parts of the mind can be harnessed.

Physical relaxation

So how do you get into this relaxed, alpha state? It starts with physical relaxation, and the basic rules are simple. Find a place where you will not be disturbed and get into a comfortable sitting or lying down position. Breathe deeply and slowly – controlled breathing alone will bring about physical relaxation and some calming of the mind. Then imagine that each part of your body feels heavy – very heavy. Work your way round the body, not just each limb but your brow, jaw and eyelids, until you start to feel pleasantly relaxed. As you become more deeply relaxed you may become aware of tingling feelings or actual vibrations, or you may get the sensation that individual limbs are no longer part of you, or your body may start to feel light rather than heavy. All these are symptoms of the relaxed, subjective state into which you are falling.

71

Mental relaxation

Your body might be relaxed but your mind might still be working overtime, thinking of a thousand and one things that are not helpful. So the next stage is to become *mentally* calm and restful as well. Take yourself, in your thoughts, to some pleasant place, or relive some enjoyable experience. Maybe there is a place you associate with tranquillity, security and restfulness. It might be an actual place, from your childhood, or from a memorable holiday, but it could be an entirely invented place. In any case, clearly visualise the place in every detail – all the sights, sounds and feelings. Savour them one by one, then enjoy the whole feeling of pleasure, safety and absolute restfulness. This mental imagery will further relax you physically, as body and mind become one, and you enter into your inner, subjective world. This is where ideas are created, problems solved, and you can engage in specific visualisation to achieve what you want. It is this relaxed state of body and mind which is associated with slow alpha brain waves. A similar effect is experienced when you gaze into a fire or at running water, such as a mountain stream. The constant movement, imagery and sound induce the relaxed alpha state. At these times the creative right brain takes over.

How long does this relaxing process take, and when is the best time to do it? With practice, you will soon be able to do it very quickly, in everyday business situations. However, at first, you may need to set aside extended times for relaxation and inner visualisation as described here. You might find it convenient to practise extended relaxation while lying in bed before going to sleep, and shorter exercises upon waking in the morning. As these techniques become more familiar, you can start to save time by using mental associations to trigger the alpha state.

Number associations

One very practical technique is to associate deepening levels of relaxation, or subjectivity, with reducing numbers. As you are doing the relaxation exercise described, count downwards, say from 100 to 1, 50 to 1, or 10 to 1, depending on the time you have. If you use this counting method each time you go through the relaxation and visualisation exercises, you will quickly start to associate falling numbers with relaxation, and very low numbers with low alpha brain waves.

An even simpler technique, partly based on the methods of José Silva, enables you to associate complete physical relaxation with the number 3. Mental calm can then be associated with the number 2 – when you have entered a pleasant mental 'place' that not only makes you feel happy and satisfied but excludes intruding thoughts. The number 1 is then reserved for an even deeper mental level, almost certain to be at alpha brain frequency, at which you are receptive to ideas from the depths of your subconscious, and also amenable to conscious suggestions and desires. At this number 1 level you can sow seeds in the subjective world that will come to fruition in the objective, external world.

How are these number associations made? In the deeply relaxed state described, and having entered the state of mental calm by clear visualisation, you should both say and see the numbers inwardly – as if on a mental screen. So, while breathing deeply and slowly, mentally repeat and visualise the number 3 three times. Then, again, while slowly breathing, the number 2. Then, in the same way, the number 1.

When you visualise the numerals, make them vivid, memorable and moving – imagine yourself writing them rather than just seeing them there in front of you. This enhances the reality of the inner images and makes for a stronger association. And use variety with each of the three

numbers. For example, you might visualise yourself painting number 3 with gold paint, maybe above the man-
telpiece. For number 2, you might use a particular coloured
marker pen on a white board – try and feel the smoothness
as you write, even smell the distinctive marker ink. For
number 1, think of another dynamic way to visualise the
numeral. If you are old enough to remember chalk on a
blackboard, you can incorporate both the sound of the
chalk on the board, and the falling chalk dust. But make
your own images, that have special meaning for you. Then,
whenever you mentally bring up that particular number
image, you will associate it with the appropriate mental state
and will immediately enter that state. This will enable you to
induce alpha waves whenever you need to – before an
important meeting, when feeling under stress, or whenever
you want to call on a more positive, creative state of mind.

In shorter times of relaxation, say first thing in the
morning, or when you have a few minutes to yourself
during the day, you can use the descending number system,
without going through the limb by limb relaxation exercises. Depending on the amount of time you have, first
count downwards from 100 to 1, 50 to 1, or 10 to 1. Again, it
helps when doing this to visualise yourself writing the
numbers – say on a flip chart. You can do this very quickly
when visualising. Then do the 3-2-1 method, using the
carefully practised, vivid images, and allowing yourself to
fall into the associated, relaxed state of mind. At this receptive level, you can programme yourself as you wish. It will
help if you bring to mind some past successful, enjoyable
memory. Positive affirmations, such as 'I am always at ease
and perform well in front of important clients', or whatever
is appropriate to your tasks and responsibilities for the day,
will also prove to be very powerful, self-fulfilling suggestions when carried out at the alpha level.

Having 'programmed yourself positively' you can return
to a wide awake state by counting slowly from 1 to 5.

Remind yourself when you get to 3 that at the count of 5 you will be wide awake, in a positive, resourceful state, ready to accomplish all you are setting out to accomplish (say this, or something similar, either out loud or to yourself). Then clicking your fingers, or using some other trigger at the count of 5, will always bring you back by association to being wide awake, and feeling good in yourself.

During these short alpha sessions after waking in the morning, you may well receive answers to problems you were addressing the day before, or that you presented to your subconscious before going to sleep. Alternatively, the answer may come in a later short session during the day. These are highly creative times, and you should get into the habit of always having a notebook and pencil at the ready to jot down ideas.

During the day, if you can find just a few undisturbed minutes you will be able to achieve alpha by the 10 to 1, then 3-2-1, method, and give yourself a real mental boost to prepare for anything you have to face.

Mandalas

Another aid to mental relaxation is the mandala. If you have seen a cross-section of a twig or a snowflake under the microscope, you will be aware of the intricate and beautiful geometric patterns that nature produces. These images are examples of mandalas – geometric patterns consisting of a series of concentric forms around one focal point. In the human eye, for example, the pupil forms the centre and the iris completes the symmetrical pattern. These patterns are also found in gemstones, flowers and seeds.

Mandalas have been used for centuries by Eastern mystics to increase concentration and to enter a receptive mental state. To use a mandala for relaxation, focus on the centre of the pattern, putting all other thoughts out of your mind. After concentrating for a few minutes, your mind

will become quieter, the usual inner dialogue and busy thoughts being replaced by a pleasant state of calm. With some practice, this technique will quickly remove unwanted thoughts so that you are in a state of relaxed alertness, in which right-brain imagery can readily be created, and ideas and insights will come easily. You can give it a try with the mandala shown.

Initially the temptation is for the eyes to wander away, and you will need to concentrate to keep your eyes focused right in the centre. The right brain is at home with shapes and pictures, and also with taking in the whole image, so it does not need to explore the different details of the image.

But the left brain wants to start analysing the shapes, counting different repetitions, and generally trying to make some logical sense out of it. With a little perseverance, your right brain will prevail, and you will enter a pleasant, relaxed state, in which the right brain can create images, and provide insights, freed from the usual predominance of left brain thinking.

6

IMAGINATION, INTUITION AND THE POWER OF DREAMS

P ROFESSIONAL MANAGERS are not expected to have feelings, at least during office hours. Imagination rarely
features on the list of desirable managerial traits. Intuition
has no place in an MBA syllabus, nor is it part of any
accepted management by objectives methodology. As a
manager, you are not supposed to say 'I feel'. You are
expected to say 'I know'.

Yet in the reality of business life many decisions are based
on intuitive feelings, and most top executives acknowledge
this. Information and analysis may be useful tools, but
when the actual decision has to be made, they are often
found wanting. Analysis does not always produce a definite
'yes' or 'no'. And in a rapidly changing business environment the information carefully gathered for analysis can
soon become dangerously out of date. What about the
information you haven't thought of getting? Or the information you weren't able to get? In such situations we call on
our intuition. But in the management environment the
language is changed: a hunch becomes 'judgement', and a
gut feeling becomes 'a considered opinion'. The problem is

how to articulate a gut feeling and still appear professional. How do you justify a right-brain insight with a left-brain report – perhaps to a left-brain boss?

It is always hard for the left-brain-trained manager to place all his or her trust in some ill-defined mysterious backwater of the mind, knowing that the decision will have to be justified in logical terms. This is hard on any would-be creative manager. Even scientists are allowed their 'eureka' moments of intuitive discovery, academics are expected to be eccentric, and self-taught entrepreneurs are permitted their gut feelings. The manager, by contrast, is constantly reined in by rationality.

Top management writer Henry Mintzberg describes the right-brain manager as: 'a holistic, intuitive thinker who revels in a climate of calculated chaos'. This hardly sounds like the text book model of a manager, but this is the sort of approach we need to take.

Understanding the psychological reality of our own intuition should give us faith in these hunches and sudden insights, and the confidence to follow them through with action.

Eureka moments

Eureka moments happen in every walk of life. They are part of the long story of human development. But they are more easily described than defined.

Whilst having a bath the ancient Greek physicist, Archimedes, pondered a question posed by the King. 'Was the royal crown made of pure gold, or was it alloyed with silver, a cheaper metal?' Noticing the way the water from his bath overflowed, Archimedes realised that since gold is denser than silver, a given weight of the yellow metal would displace less water. Overjoyed by his discovery, he ran naked into the street shouting 'Eureka' (I have found it). He then demonstrated his discovery to the King, proving that his crown had indeed been fashioned from alloy.

Artists have long drawn on their intuitive powers. Both Robert Fulton, inventor of the steamboat, and Samuel Morse, inventor of the telegraph, started life as artists, but were led elsewhere by intuition. From the imagination of sculptor Lazlo Biro emerged the ballpoint pen.

Athletes, similarly, are familiar with these special moments. Basketball star Larry Bird says 'It's scary. When I'm at my best I can do just about anything I want and no one can stop me. I feel like I'm in total control of everything.' Sometimes he will turn away, elated, from the net, knowing before the ball drops through that he has scored a goal.

These ecstatic 'mountain top' experiences are rare and should be savoured. They are frequently described as coming from 'outside' the individual – a gift from the gods.

Scientists have also described such moments with particular eloquence. Take this experience:

For me, the best analogy is what sometimes happens when you're sailing a round-bottomed boat in a strong wind. Normally, the hull stays down in the water, with the frictional drag greatly limiting the speed of the boat. But in high wind, every once in a while the hull lifts out of the water, and the drag goes instantly to zero. It feels like a great hand has suddenly grabbed hold and flings you across the surface like a skimming stone. It's called planing.

I've planed in my scientific career only on a few occasions and then for only a few seconds. Einstein and Darwin probably planed for hours at a time. The years of details at my desk have been bearable because of those moments. I could use a lot more of them.

Joseph Heller, top management writer and editor of *Management Today* for a number of years, writes: 'I don't understand the process of imagination, though I know that I am very much at its mercy. I feel like these ideas are floating around in the air and they pick me to settle on. The ideas come to me. I don't produce them at will.'

Entrepreneurs unashamedly act on instinct and 'gut feelings'. This is partly because their work usually requires them to take fast, risky decisions and they rarely have time to gather all the information. However, many of them also naturally choose to rely on intuition – a 'sixth sense' that enables them to spot winning business opportunities.

The American multi-millionaire and presidential candidate Ross Perot has followed his gut feelings through a whole series of successful business ventures. He sees intuition as 'knowing your business . . . being able to bring to bear on a situation everything you've seen, felt, tasted and experienced in an industry.'

The artist, the writer, the entrepreneur are all used to calling on their intuition. It is the corporate executive, the modern-day manager, who needs a little help in identifying, encouraging and trusting these special feelings. At whatever level of management, we need to understand how the brain constantly delves into the subconscious to make sense of disparate bits of knowledge and experience, which it then fuses with new information, to produce the 'eureka' solution. To do this, we need to explore the limitless power of right-brain imagination.

The power of the imagination

Imagination has been described as the greatest force in the universe. Many great advances in science, medicine and social welfare have come about through individuals with great imagination. Science, like management, is concerned with facts. Drawing on formal logic and based on so-called 'scientific method', it might be expected to utilise only left-brain skills. But although much of the routine research involves painstaking recording and analysis – as do many aspects of management – this is far from being the whole story. The greatest advances, both in science and other fields, have occurred when human imagination has been free to roam at will.

Einstein for example, discovered his theory of relativity not seated at his desk, but while lying on a hill one summer day. As he looked up with half-closed eyes, according to his own account, the sun dappled through his eyelashes, breaking into thousands of tiny sunbeams. He wondered what it would be like to go for a ride on one of those sunbeams, and imagined himself going on a journey through the universe. His imagination took him to a place where his formal training in physics told him he should not be. Concerned about this, he went back to his blackboard, and, believing his imagination to be more correct than his formal training, worked out a new mathematics to explain the truth of what his brain had told him.

Kekulé, a German chemist, also made a momentous discovery by using his creative imagination. After spending much time in the laboratory trying to identify the molecular structure of benzene, he would go home and sit in front of the fire, half awake, half asleep, letting the patterns of the coal and flames inspire him. He explained how he finally discovered the benzene ring:

I turned my chair to the fire and dozed. Again the atoms were gambolling before my eyes. This time the smaller groups kept modestly in the background. My mental eye, rendered more acute by repeated visions of this kind, could now distinguish larger structures, in manifold conformation; long rows sometimes more closely fitted together, all turning and twisting in snakelike motion. But look! What was that? One of the snakes had seized hold of its own tail and the form whirled mockingly before my eyes. As if by a flash of lightning I awoke.

This power of the imagination is too important to be excluded from your armoury for there is no area of management that will not benefit from the creative insights your imagination can provide.

Left- and right-brain harmony

Once they discover the power of the imagination, many people fall into the trap of treating imagination and reason (or logical left-brain thinking) in an either-or way. In fact the human brain functions best when the left and right brains are working in harmony. And real creativity is only found in such whole brain partnerships. What is noticeable about the many outstanding stories of great scientific advances throughout history is the way people combined imagination and intuition with careful, reasoned analysis. It was the partnership of right and left brain that made the crucial difference. Einstein was able to transform his dream into provable formulae. Edison's light bulbs had to be manufactured and made to work reliably. And any successful entrepreneur has to convert his or her ideas into bottom-line results.

So how does imagination mix with 'ordinary' thinking? And need there be any conflict? Sometimes they seem to be poles apart – laboriously, logically thinking out the solution to an intractable problem, or making the easy, intuitive leap that seems to produce an answer from nothing. At other times they simply appear to be different ways in which the mind works, used for different purposes, like a hammer and a saw. A distraught parent imagines all sorts of terrible things have happened to a child who is late coming home. Far too upset to think rationally, and work out the probability of such things actually happening, he or she is the passive victim of a feverishly active imagination. Likewise, the habitual worrier displays a powerfully negative use of imagination. In these cases a bit of left-brain reasoning would certainly help the person put their worries into perspective.

Sometimes, however, it seems as if left- and right-brain ways of thinking are inextricably interwoven. A man is reading a scientific account of the geology and topology of an Indonesian island. Whilst taking in every factual detail of the account, he fills out the description with mental pictures of the scenery, the inhabitants and what it would feel like to be there. He is both thinking, as a scientist, and imagining – bringing to life a subject he enjoys. His thinking and imagining work happily side by side, for different but complementary purposes.

To give another example, a historian or detective needs to be scrupulous in his gathering of evidence and chronological detail. But he also has to bring these many pieces of information together in a creative, intuitive way in order to reach a conclusion. Reason and imagination are part of the same process of enquiry. Details must be analysed with imagination, and imaginative insights must be tested with logic and common sense.

Making room for intuition and imagination

If imagination is the source of so many brilliant ideas and

insights, how can we access its power to become better managers? One of the golden rules is that we need *time* to think and reflect.

The managing director of a large company in the oil industry told me that he spent some three hours every day thinking. This, he said, was where all his successes came from, where his ideas were born and his best solutions emerged. At his level he insisted this was a vital part of his job. Fortunately his status and position enabled him to make this use of his time. His office was on the ground floor of the main building, next to the main reception area, and visible to all the hundreds of employees coming and going. Everybody knew the boss spent half his time asleep! But the results of his imagination and leadership skill had gained him the respect he deserved.

He explained his philosophy to me. He had large numbers of first-class staff to carry out every aspect of the work of the corporation. There was plenty of analysis, plenty of rational decision-making, more than enough left-brain thinking, structured into every part of the operation. The person who was expected, and paid, to do something extra – not just another level, another rubber stamp on the same process – was the chief executive. Somebody had to think about the future. Somebody had to come up with new strategies to fend off the competition, and gain new markets. Somebody had to lead while the others managed.

In a more junior management role it is unlikely that you could allocate as much as three hours a day simply to thinking. This is not to undervalue the place of thinking in every manager's schedule but simply to acknowledge that few companies have yet recognised, let alone harnessed, the enormous creative potential in their people.

There are many other opportunities, however, for thinking within day-to-day managerial activities. A number of managers said they used the time spent driving to and from work or between business appointments for creative thinking. By driving on 'autopilot' – not consciously thinking about it – they found it easy to be fully absorbed in what was on their mind. The home to office drive was often used as a winding up or winding down time so that they were able to give their best both at work and at home.

In some cases the journey was a carefully structured time for thinking, in a right-brain, free-wheeling mode. The managing director of a group of fashion stores and factories told me about his system. He had to make a weekly visit to a plant in Wales. He deliberately chose a slower, more relaxing route that took him about three hours – far longer than the fastest route. Setting off quite unprepared for the many issues and decisions he knew he would have to face, he would reach the plant fully prepared with questions for his local managers, embryonic solutions to many of the problems he guessed would be raised, and insights into longer-term challenges. What came from the depths of his subconscious on these long journeys must have sounded like carefully rehearsed and analysed solutions to the plant management team. Furthermore, these intuitions had been proved right time and time again. This manager knew the importance of imagination and intuition, and actually went to the trouble of making time for it to happen. The weekly three-hour journey to Wales had become a valued personal management resource.

Other productive right-brain times were when shaving, showering, or doing any routine tasks that could be carried out 'without thinking'. One senior engineering manager associated his time shaving each morning not just with moments of insight, but, by seeing himself in the mirror, with the honesty he felt was vital in any management role. Each day, in more ways than one, he 'faced himself'. To this manager, times of intuition were also important for self-development and understanding.

The thoughts we get at these times may be fleeting and incomplete so it is important to record them in some way.

Scribble down the idea, or partial idea, so that it will be there when you need it. One manager found his carphone useful for this – he would ring an appropriate colleague and pass on whatever occurred to him at that moment. Another chief executive chose not to have a carphone precisely because he valued the uninterrupted thinking time he got when driving. You will need to work out your own system. But remember that the best ideas come when you are relaxed – during the night, even through dreams, or first thing in the morning – only to be forgotten by the time your reach the office. Always keep a notepad or dictaphone handy.

Applying intuition at work

I have found plenty of evidence of practical ways in which managers use their intuitive thinking. For instance, the chairman and managing director of a large building company told me about an occasion when he entered a large building site and instinctively knew that the value of work in progress was well below the actual figure he had been given. The scale and complexity of the site made it almost impossible for any such calculation to be made other than by a full physical measurement and costing. Although his intuitive remark was at first refuted by the site manager, sure enough it turned out that he was right. Far more than long experience was at work here. Few managers with similar experience can make such judgements. Only the holistic right brain can perform such feats.

This particular manager was an expert in his field, of course, and had grown up in the building industry. In other cases judgements are questioned by non-experts. For example, I met a senior manager, from a sales background, who dared to ask the question 'Can we save tax?' He was running a joint venture of two multi-nationals that, as such, had to be separately registered as a company, and was liable to tax. He wondered whether the tax losses of one of the parent companies could be used to offset his company's liabilities. The answer came back negative. With no knowledge of the technicalities, he instinctively felt this was wrong, and pursued his questioning. Eventually, after some persistence, the parent company experts conceded that by treating the company as a consortium, offsetting tax losses were, indeed, available. Substantial tax relief was received, producing large cash flow benefits. It is easy to underestimate this power of intuition, appearing as it does as persistence or experience or, with hindsight, just 'common sense'.

Intuition applied to people

Most of the intuition I have learned of seems to involve people and the 'chemistry' between them. For instance, the final decision about making an appointment from a short-list of job candidates is often based on this undefined chemistry – an instinctive like or dislike, or perhaps the ability to 'see' the person working within the culture of the company and existing management team. In one company a fitter had left to start up a family business, which failed, and he later returned, hoping to get his job back. It seemed he had been a somewhat disruptive character, and there had been some relief when he went. The foreman's recommendation not to re-hire him was unequivocal. But the then senior manager responsible, after a brief interview, felt he should be taken on. There was 'just something about him' that made him want to give the man another chance. Against all advice to the contrary, the man got his job back. He settled in well, started doing extra training, and eventually became a key player in the company's computer-aided design programme. By any standards he was an asset to the company, and one of the best appointments this manager, now the managing director, ever made.

These intuitive 'people decisions' often involve clients and suppliers as well as staff. A remarkable right-brain decision was made by a sales manager negotiating a contract in the Far East. He had scheduled two days with the buyer following a day with the company's agent. Some urgent business had cropped up back in the UK that might require leaving on the second day, but this was not nearly as important as successfully negotiating the contract. On being introduced to the buyer on the morning of the second day, he (the buyer) *smiled*. On the basis of that smile, the manager made a decision to end the negotiations at the end of that same day, and fly back the same evening! He had assessed the buyer to be the sort of character who would string out discussions to the very end, not coming to any agreement until late the following day. This would not, he felt, have given any advantage to the selling firm, nor would it have suited his own style of negotiation. So on that flimsiest of gut feelings, based on a smile, the sales manager arranged to fly out that evening – to his great relief, securing the contract shortly before departure; a contract vital both to him and the company.

Intuition into profit

At a time when I was involved in property development I was listening to the car radio and some mention was made of the new town of Skelmersdale. After being almost a ghost town for many years, it was apparently about to experience economic growth, much like Milton Keynes and other developments. I had no interest in or knowledge of Skelmersdale, knowing only vaguely that it was somewhere in the North-West of England. Nevertheless I had a strange urge to drive up there and look for some properties. Soon I did just that, and made substantial profits on three separate deals. What had made me buy those properties?

Well, I had been doing some doctoral research which plotted house price rises moving from London outwards through the country on a predictable 'ripple'. Sooner or later, I knew that prices in the North-West would rise too. I had also been receiving monthly building society statistics, and I had noticed that the North-West was just about ready to take off – not yet having been affected by widespread property inflation. So, lurking somewhere in my sub-conscious were the data from the recent doctoral thesis and the building society statistics concerning the North-West. All it took was that casual reference to Skelmersdale, long-buried knowledge in my mind said was in that part of the country, and the association was made. Three otherwise totally meaningless bits of information were brought to-gether, against enormous statistical odds, by cross-association and in accordance with goals I had clearly envisioned. This is the entrepreneur's hunch – demystified, but no less remarkable. This is the scientist's eureka, the writer's muse, the special insight which seems to rise mirac-ulously into consciousness when we least expect it.

Every manager needs to draw on these mysterious vapours from the subconscious from time to time. Logic and analysis can take you so far but what ultimately makes a decision the right one? Will the appraisal technique or decision-making model take you over that last, all-important hurdle? Can you really take into account all the external factors?

Intuition is above all an ephemeral quality, and we can easily let it slip away. The late business philosopher R. Buckmaster Fuller, designer of the geodesic dome, called intuition 'cosmic fishing', but warned that 'once you feel a nibble, you've got to hook the fish'. How many revolution-ary, life-enhancing ideas languish in the mute, subterra-nean caverns of the subconscious mind, having failed to reach the light of day? If we can only find the confidence to make these intuitive decisions we will almost always be proved right in the long term.

Unleashing the imagination

Apart from making time for these insights, and being more ready to trust them, how can we use imagination to increase our effectiveness as managers? Well, we need to begin by exercising the imaginative, intuitive aspect of our brains. For many people, lack of use has withered and atrophied the imagination. Like a weakened muscle or limb, it needs gentle exercise to reawaken it.

First make sure you will not be interrupted for a little while. Then work through different parts of your body, relaxing them one by one and breathing gently. Now close your eyes and turn them upward about twenty degrees, looking some distance away rather than just in front of your eyes.

Try visualising your name spelled out in front of you, as if on a screen. Can you make it look as though it has been written on a blackboard? Can you see it being rubbed out? Now imagine yourself writing it with chalk on the same blackboard. This time you will see the hand and the movement as well as the finished name. Did you hear the squeak of the chalk? Could you smell the chalk dust? How was that? If it was not possible at all, start again, but make sure you are nice and relaxed, and can concentrate fully. This time try and visualise a simple shape – a square, then a triangle, then a circle. If the images are indistinct and fleeting, just persevere, and with practice you will get better.

If you had no difficulty with those exercises, have a go at introducing some colours. Why not a different colour for each letter of your name? Can you easily visualise drawing with a coloured marker pen on a white board? Now what sort of room are you in? Explore the room and see its furnishings and other details. Make the walls bright yellow. Is anybody else there? Why not put someone there, anyone you wish, even a person you have never met personally but have seen on television? What sounds can you hear? Listen carefully, and you will pick up distant sounds from outside, or from an adjacent room. Make the sounds in your imagination stronger than those actual sounds that try to slip into your hearing.

Those readers who are struggling can try some different sounds such as church bells, the music accompanying the television news, the voice of your spouse or a close friend or relation. Start with familiar, easy things, then progress to more imaginative exercises. The mind is a great unexplored ocean, full of fantastic images and surprises.

Now try some 'mental movement'. In your imagination, do some walking and running, and a range of exercises. If you like playing a certain sport then rehearse some of the movements in your mind. If you are a swimmer, feel the sensation of cold water on your body, and the pressure of the water. You can use these techniques to improve your abilities in sport. Some people find it easier to imagine sensations. What about stroking a cat or a dog, or a horse? What does it feel like to run your hands against the nap of the fur? Try dipping your hand in ice-cold water. Feel both the coldness and the wetness.

When you are ready, have a go at smelling and tasting. Can you smell petrol or freshly baked bread? Can you taste vinegar and a hot milk drink? When you can easily imagine these senses you are well on the way to being able to use your mind for positive, constructive purposes. The imagery will get stronger and stronger with regular use. With practice the visualisation will become hardly distinguishable from the real senses, especially when you are in a relaxed, receptive 'alpha' state.

All of this you can then apply to any business situation. Think of your top three problems as a manager, then imagine what it would be like if they were solved. How would the people involved behave differently? How would you feel? Stretch your imagination to see, hear and feel in detail the new situation. By doing so you are creating a new, inner reality, and this is where change begins.

What about opening up your mind to new business opportunities – say, new or enhanced products or services, and new markets? Or you can be equally creative in thinking of ways to save costs. Although group brainstorming has traditionally been used to unleash new ideas, you have the ability to stimulate this prolific creativity personally. But rather than just come up with a list of ideas, you can imagine and manipulate whole new scenarios – alternative scenarios – in vivid detail. You will learn to feel what is right, and what will work, by experiencing it subjectively. This is the visionary skill of great leaders and innovators that we can all cultivate and use.

Set aside some time each day to relax, explore your subjective world, and practise controlling your thoughts. Then start using your imagination and trusting your instincts and insights in day-to-day business and personal life.

Harnessing dream power

Even the most analytical, non-creative manager spends many hours each week in extreme right-brain mode – when he or she is asleep. Everyone dreams for several periods each night, and these periods are characterised by rapid eye movement (REM). If a patient is awakened during REM sleep, he or she will invariably recall a dream. So we all have dreams, but some of us regularly recall our dreams, and others do not. However, not surprisingly, right-brain thinkers tend to recall their dreams more readily than predominantly left-brain thinkers. Dreaming is, of course, very much a right-brain activity, having its own visual imagery which is not usually understandable in terms of language or logic. Because of this, recalling and describing a dream involves transferring imagery in waking consciousness from the right brain to the left. So dreaming is a rather special state of mind, and a very special use of the right brain.

The purpose of dreaming

Why do we dream? And is there any practical use to which we can put this universal, nightly phenomenon? It seems that dreaming is a form of mental housekeeping, as essential as maintaining physical health and hygiene. We have already seen how a conscious problem seems to be handed over to the subconscious, and in due course some solution emerges back into the conscious, as an insight or revelation. Many managers find that these answers frequently come first thing in the morning, following conscious, perhaps intensive thought before going to sleep. So it seems that there is a great deal of truth in the familiar expression 'sleeping on a problem'. Apart from this problem-solving role, dreaming has other, even more important functions.

As well as the known problems we face day by day, there are other subconscious conflicts that our minds are always trying to resolve. There are vulnerable areas in each of us, to do with aspects of our personality perhaps, and deep-rooted beliefs about ourselves. Any incongruence or mismatch between experience or beliefs we have already stored away and what comes to us as new experience, seems to set up tensions; and it is these tensions that surface in our dreams. Present tension, or the emotion associated with it, makes us want to search out feelings or images that shed light on the situation and bring better order. This healing, cleansing process can only be achieved during dreaming. It is, if you like, a mental self-cleaning mechanism that we could not do without.

The strange events and images we recall from our dreams seem to relate to the *process* that is going on – the searching, classifying and rearranging of data to make sense – in the same way as a librarian puts all the books back in the right order at the end of each day. The language of dreaming is not for conscious (left-brain) consumption – the sequential, logical left brain could never cope with this massive data search and classification. Instead, a different, holistic operating system is needed, and this is provided by the right brain. The strange images from the past that appear in our dreams – sometimes going right back to childhood – illustrate the total search that is going on to find the required solution. And what we later recall as bizarre, nonsensical imagery all seems to be part of a special right-brain mode of inner communication.

However imprecise our understanding of dreaming, its significance is becoming more and more apparent, for three main reasons. Firstly, our dreams are often relevant to active issues in our lives. They handle the problems we face in what seems to be an optimal way. Secondly, dreams are able to mobilise pertinent feelings and information from the past, memories that are completely out of reach of the conscious left brain. And thirdly, dreams reveal the unvarnished truth about us. Whatever the limitations of dream understanding and interpretation, we are dealing with a frighteningly truthful part of ourselves.

Making use of your dreams

Can we use our dreams in any specific, planned way? In its simplest form, dream control involves *asking* your dreams to help solve a particular problem! We have already explored ways of handing over problems to the right brain and later receiving the insights that solve them, but when this happens during unconscious sleep rather than conscious waking time, it takes on a more mystical guise.

However, although not conscious during sleep, we are certainly *aware*. Some people are able to wake up more or less as desired, without the use of alarm clocks, according to some sort of mental self-programming method that operates during sleep. A mother can sleep through all manner of noises but seems to be programmed to wake at her baby's slightest whimper. Similarly, you are likely to wake if someone calls your name during sleep, but not if they call another name. So we know that the brain is active and aware, though not conscious of what is going on around us.

How do you give a dream instruction? Do it in your alpha state before going to sleep. Use the 3-2-1 method and the same sort of imagery already described to visualise the problem clearly, and simply request the answer – out loud, if you wish. While you are at the receptive alpha level, also request that you wake up at the right time to recall the dream. And request that you will be able to understand the meaning of the dream sufficiently to solve your problem. Don't expect to achieve full control straight away. Like all mental techniques, you will need to practise each stage over a period of time in order to become proficient.

Start off by just recalling regularly your dreams (any dreams) if you do not already do so, by instruction from your alpha level. Next, start to address specific problems, and ask to recall the dreams that are 'handling' these. Then proceed to request insights into the meaning of the dreams, so that you can apply them to the problems. Whatever you do, do not go to sleep without a pencil and notepad at the ready. Recalled dreams can be very elusive, and there is nothing more frustrating than knowing you had some earth-shattering revelation but forgetting what it was.

Dream insights can be extremely specific. For example, one managing director was faced with a subsidiary company that was making a substantial loss. The name of a client of the company came to him the morning after he had thought deeply about the problem, which he vaguely linked with a dream he had had that night (although he did not often recall his dreams). But, as well as the name, he had the strange idea of terminating business with the client, by letting their contract lapse. The name in question had not been seen in any reports for many months. And that is exactly what the dream process had unlocked – the level of business with this client had fallen right off. On checking the records, they were also found to have a poor payment record. All these factors, together with large discounts given at the last negotiation based on projected turnover, were a recipe for bottom line losses. In short, the company would be better off without this client's business. Amazingly, this uncanny, very specific dream revelation was later well supported by the facts of the situation, and proved to be a shrewd business decision by any standards. More than this, the same principle was applied to other clients, most of whom responded to the implicit threat of losing their contracts by increasing the level of their business and paying more promptly. Profitability was thus regained!

Like using your imagination, you can condition yourself to recall dreams and use them. The Senoi tribe deep in the jungle of the Malay Peninsula have a strong tradition of dreaming, which is inculcated into their children from a very early age. Everyone in the tribe remembers their dreams, and the dreams are used for suggestions for the tribe, personal development (as we would describe it) and practical daily guidance. As with other right-brain functions, we in the West have given dreaming a very low value in our culture. Yet, as managers, the surprising originality of dreams should remind us again and again of the creativity that is a feature of the human mind. Understanding and using these powers is the secret of personal and management success.

7

REMEMBERING

JUST LIKE any other feature of the mind, remembering
does not require special brain hardware, or some hereditary gift. You do not have to be a special person to exercise
apparently supernatural feats of memory, any more than a
circus juggler has to be born with that gift. It comes with
knowledge, application and a bit of hard work. But the
benefits are well worth the time and effort involved.

I was once standing in a hotel lift when a lady entered at
an intermediate floor. Instantly she greeted me by name
and entered into small talk about how my company, which
she also remembered, was doing. I was embarrassed at not
being able to remember her name – and worse, what
company she represented and where on earth we had met.
But my embarrassment was more than matched by how
impressed and flattered I was that she had remembered my
name and face from a single business meeting several years
earlier. Any salesman knows that if you can remember little
Johnny's hobby, and the fact that Mary will have had her
operation, you hardly need a sales pitch. The ability to use
your memory gives you a massive head start over the
competition.

Indeed, it can work wonders in almost any management
situation. It is far more impressive to give a presentation
without reference to notes, or be instantly familiar with the
names and functions of clients at an important negotiation

meeting, or show a thorough knowledge of all the personal data on a member of staff you are appraising. With the aid of a few simple techniques, you can access your virtually unlimited capacity to retain and recall information.

Rate your own memory

How do you rate your memory? Some people seem to excel in certain subject areas – such as a hobby or special interest. Others seem to remember certain kinds of information, like birthdays or car registration numbers, but otherwise might have minds like sieves. Some can vividly recollect events from many years ago, but are quite absent-minded on a day-to-day level. There is no simple yardstick for memory efficiency.

But in almost every case, there is ample room for improvement. And as far as your management role is concerned, there are plenty of ways in which a better memory can be converted into greater effectiveness in achieving company objectives, and career and personal advancement.

First, let us look at the size of the problem. Do you recognise any of these signs of memory inefficiency?

- Forgetting where you put things.
- Forgetting to take things with you.
- Forgetting the name of a colleague you used to know very well.
- Forgetting the point you are making – having a mental block.
- Forgetting important personal information, like telephone numbers, car registration numbers, or your spouse's birthday.
- Getting temporarily lost in a town or building you have been to many times.

- Asking the same question twice in a short space of time.
- Having difficulty mastering some new electronic gadget, skill or game that others seem to take in their stride.
- Losing the thread of a story or newspaper article.

Do any of these ring true? Do they occur rarely, or about once a month, once a week, or even daily?

If you rate yourself badly, do not be concerned. If you are a busy person with a lot of demands on your time and attention, you are bound to forget more – you have more things to forget. The important thing is that everyone can improve their memory.

Principles of better memory

Over the years there has been a great deal of research into memory, and how we can improve it. In the 1870s Hermann Ebbinghaus, a German philosopher, conducted experiments on himself, learning endless strings of nonsense syllables and testing himself rigorously at predetermined intervals to measure what he had remembered and forgotten. His and other research has established some useful principles for the would-be memory improver.

Firstly, the speed at which information can be taken in by the mind is never the problem. Our senses and brain can absorb vast amounts of data – even subconsciously, as is the case with high speed reading or subliminal messages. The problems invariably arise with retention and recall.

Secondly, the brain's capacity to store information is, to all intents and purposes, unlimited. In computer terms, there is no danger of running out of hard disk space. How much information we can take in and how quickly, have never been an issue. It all boils down to how easily information can be *recalled*. So the techniques for improving memory concern the way information is stored, and the way it is recalled – the software programs you can design and run rather than the brain hardware you are born with.

Little and often

A few other helpful principles have emerged over the years. For instance, your ability to recall stored information is largely dependent on the time you have spent putting it in. This is known as the 'Total Time Hypothesis.'

But it is by no means the whole story. Another hypothesis says that short, frequent periods of memory practice give better results, per unit of time, than a long session. Sadly, these basic principles have not yet been acknowledged by many in the field of management training. One multinational company for whom I conducted training ran an intensive three-month induction course for graduate trainee managers. The subjects I covered were scheduled close to the end of the three-month period, and the trainees were simply too drained and data-drunk to absorb anything more. Any learning process – which invariably involves memory – will benefit from the little and often principle.

Learning at the best rate

Another memory principle involves the rate at which we learn. For example, is it better to learn a list of foreign vocabulary by fully learning each word before moving on to another, or by repeating the whole list so that there is a gap (as long as the time taken to read the whole list) between each word recited? The answer is that initially the words must be close enough to ensure rapid memorising, but as words are remembered they just need to be re-tested at increasingly longer intervals. This principle can be applied to many learning processes. As an illustration, the pattern for memorising four French words would go as follows:

TEACHER SAYS:	LEARNER SAYS:
stable – l'ecurie	
stable?	l'ecurie
horse – le cheval	
horse?	le cheval
stable?	l'ecurie
horse?	le cheval
grass – l'herbe	
grass?	l'herbe
stable?	l'ecurie
horse?	le cheval
grass?	l'herbe
church – l'eglise	
church?	l'eglise
grass?	l'herbe
church?	l'eglise
stable?	l'ecurie
grass?	l'herbe
horse?	le cheval

Whenever the learner gets a word wrong it should be presented after a shorter delay. If a word is got right, the delay can be increased. In this way learning will be optimal, and, importantly, the learner will not lose heart by repeatedly getting wrong answers. This memory principle has, not surprisingly, been incorporated into computer-based methods of learning in an attempt to achieve optimum memory retention. Like the other memory principles described here, it is really no more than common sense – but not too common in the world of education and training.

Motivation to learn

The motivation to remember and learn is probably an even more important factor than the technique used. Interestingly, it has been shown that there is no marked effect on the quality of recall when rewards or punishments are used with human subjects. However, as any school teacher knows, the offer of a reward will mean that the learner *spends more time* on the learning and for this reason (according to the Total Time Hypothesis) is bound to remember more. If I asked you to memorise a list of towns for a penny each, and a list of flowers for a pound each, I know which you would do better on. You would not waste your time on the penny list at all. Inducements affect the time and effort you put in, not the internal memory process. But, as we shall see, there are plenty of ways to improve that process.

The importance of meaning

The material that Ebbinghaus chose to remember last century was specifically chosen because it did *not* have meaning. In order to avoid any distortion in the case of familiar syllables that were easier to recall, he taught himself nonsense syllables such as JIH, BAZ, FUB, or YOX. But, in practice, recall is markedly improved if the words, or other data, have meaning. More specifically, and this takes us back to right-brain skills, information is best remembered if it can be translated into mental pictures or *visualised*.

You can easily test this memory principle. Spend thirty seconds trying to learn each of these two lists, then see how many of the ten items in each list you can remember.

List 1:

book, field, snow, hat, cow, chimney, curtains, railway, reservoir, carpenter

List 2:

pride, hope, tranquillity, annoyance, care, quietness, law, disobedience, pain, worth.

Which list did you score best on? Most people find words in the first list easier to remember because they are real things, rather than just abstract concepts, which are difficult to visualise. I call such words 'picturable'.

But even the first list is not easy to remember, because such a list still has no overall meaning. It demands dull, mechanical rote-learning, of which most people have negative school memories. If, however, the list went:

dawn, walk, storm, fell, rescue, home, grateful

a possible meaning could be detected, at least enough to help the memory, as the imagination can picture the words and also fill the gaps to create an overall story. For this reason such a list is much easier to remember.

If a fuller meaning is given, then ten different words can instantly be remembered, and subsequently recalled:

The black cat sat in front of the blazing fire.

In this case the words (now a sentence) become something more – a picture or scene, an image of a cat in front of the fire. The right brain revels in this sort of task. It enjoys dealing with images as much as the left brain enjoys dealing with language. In each case there needs to be *meaning*, but right-brain imagery is more powerful than language when it comes to remembering.

Sentences are not the only way to give words meaning. Classification is another. Your departmental filing system probably has broad subject headings, described by one or two words, further broken down into words denoting sub-classifications, then possibly further broken down into individual files. The hierarchical structure of those file headings makes them more meaningful and therefore more useful. In the same way a meaningful structure improves our ability to remember.

Have a look at the following two sets of words:

SET 1: MINERALS

metals			*stones*	
RARE	COMMON	ALLOYS	PRECIOUS	MASONRY
platinum	aluminium	bronze	sapphire	limestone
silver	copper	steel	emerald	granite
gold	lead	brass	diamond	marble

SET 2:

pine elm pansy garden wild banyan plants
delphinium conifers dandelion redwood palm
ash violet daisy tropical chestnut flowers
spruce lupin buttercup trees deciduous mango
willow rose

Which set would you prefer to memorise? The first list is far easier because it has more meaning, though a close look at the second list will show that a similar sort of classification could have been applied. Structured, meaningful information is more easily understood and recalled, and this gives us important clues as to how best to present filing systems, reports, or any list or document that we need to become familiar with.

Imagery techniques

Another way to help the memory process is by using visual imagery, and this is where we call on the special strengths of the right brain. Mental pictures are considerably more memorable than words and language, and account for nearly all the outstanding feats of memory that we often hear about.

Suppose you need to remember the two words 'clock' and 'teapot'. As these are picturable words, you will have no difficulty with imagining them. But to create some overall meaning, you somehow need to link the two words together. If they rhymed, or were opposites like chalk and cheese, or were linked like the names of two mountains, it would be easy, of course. But these two words do not have any obvious connection. So you make one by using your imagination. Think of any situation which might link the two. You might visualise a grandfather clock and in place of the pendulum weight there hangs a teapot. Or out of the teapot pour lots of little clocks! It does not matter what the association is. The more unusual and bizarre the better, as your memory store will not have a ready-made pigeon-hole for it, and will therefore give it extra attention. Moreover, the right brain is particularly adept at both creating and recalling mental images. The fact that the association is a nonsensical one does not matter. Meaning need not be sensible, rational left-brain meaning – just meaning. Your right brain does not pass judgement; it accepts the pictures for what they are worth.

Let us put this principle into practice with a simple exercise. This technique can be used by anyone, including those who got a poor score in the earlier memory test, or who do not consider themselves to have a good visual imagination.

First, limber up by thinking of three or four words and linking them with bizarre visual images, as before. You will be surprised at your ability to remember.

Now look at the following random words:

knight college child farm bridge cheque bottle sledge computer cliff

Visualise an image associated with each word, but link each image in some way so as to make an ongoing story that links all ten words. The images, and the associations, must be as unusual and memorable as you can make them, and they must make sense to you. They must come from *your* imagination. Here's an example:

> *I see a knight in shining armour riding up to the college where he frightens a child who runs to a nearby farm where the farmer is playing bridge but stops to draw a cheque which he puts into a bottle and ties the bottle to a sledge which runs down a slope and hits a computer which topples over the cliff.*

You must come up with your own silly story, which is bound to be different to mine as the words will have different associations, and you will remember all the words, in the right order. After thinking about something quite different for an hour you will still be able to rattle them off just as well as when you first memorised them, because the visual images are so easily recalled. Try it. The simple rule is to *visualise clearly* the images you want to portray in the story, and those images have to be as ridiculous and memorable as you can make them. Visualise also the story connection between each word-picture.

Later on, if you cannot recall the start of the story (which will immediately bring it all back to you) then you might visualise the number 1 or the letter A in some memorable association with the knight, so that when you want to recall the beginning, you mentally imagine the A or number 1 which will immediately bring to mind the first word-picture. You can just as easily recite the words from the end, by running the story backwards. If you start with any word in the middle you can still recall all the words if you associate the last word with the first, to make a loop – for example, the computer might land on the unwary knight who gallops off to the college. You have created a memory pattern which can be instantly recalled, and recited from any point, forwards or backwards. By using right-brain *imagery*, rather than left-brain *words*, you can memorise the material in a fraction of the time it would normally take by rote-learning, and the information will be retained much longer.

This method can be used by anyone to recall scores of otherwise unmemorable facts or words. Like many managers, you probably often write out lists of 'things to do' the following day. Although there is no need to commit these to memory, it will increase your efficiency if you can avoid having to refer to a written list at regular intervals. It will also be good practice for times when you need to use the memory device seriously, such as when making a verbal presentation, or conducting an important meeting.

There is *no limit* to the number of words you can store and recall in this way. Once a clear image has been created, and an association from one word to the next by means of some continuing story, your mind will do the rest. It simply cannot forget a vivid, perhaps bizarre image. But do not be tricked into disbelief by your left brain! Trust and use your mind to the full.

Peg systems

Another simple but very effective memory aid is the peg system. There are many versions but I shall describe just one.

First memorise the following words that can be associated with the numbers 1 to 10 by rhyming:

one – **bun**
two – **shoe**
three – **tree**
four – **door**
five – **hive**
six – **sticks**
seven – **heaven**
eight – **gate**
nine – **wine**
ten – **hen**

You will quickly memorise these. Usually the rhyming is enough to make the association, but if you need to, you can make a further visual connection. For example, the bun could be in the shape of a number 1, the shoe might have size 2 stamped on it, and so on. Remember that you need to form your own unique images and associations.

Once you are familiar with the peg words, try and link, by imagery again, the following ten words with the ten number images, 'bun', 'shoe', 'tree' etc.

1 **desk**
2 **house**
3 **photograph**
4 **spaceship**
5 **shirt**
6 **grass**
7 **steam**
8 **finger**
9 **fairy**
10 **iceberg**

Create the associations yourself – for example, a giant bun on a desk, a big shoe used as a house, a life-size photograph of a tree, and so on. The same rules about bizarre connections apply as in the previous technique. Then, by working through the numbers from 1 to 10, you will immediately remember the linking peg word, which will in turn trigger the new word in the right order. There is no need to connect the images in a story, as the numbers provide the sequence. The advantage of this system is that once you have remembered the peg words, which takes a few minutes, if you use the system regularly they will stay with you for life, becoming as instinctive as $2 \times 2 = 4$.

You can also reverse the process to remember important numbers. Let us say your cash card number, 3688, gives the peg words 'tree', 'sticks', 'gate', 'gate'. So you simply need to think of a tree chopped into sticks to make two gates. Now have a go at using the peg words to remember some numbers or birthdays you would like to commit painlessly to long-term memory.

Names and faces

Other visual memory techniques can be used to remember people's names and faces. This can be invaluable in some jobs and social situations, and particularly so for managers responsible for a number of staff, and meeting many clients, suppliers and other more casual acquaintances. Forgetting someone's name a few seconds after you've been introduced to them gives a very bad impression. Conversely, clients and staff are never more flattered and impressed than when you show mastery of their names and personal and social backgrounds. They appreciate the trouble you must have gone to and the value you place on them as individuals.

Harry Lorayne, who wrote the book *Remembering People*, would remember hundreds of people at a party or conference, having been quickly introduced to them at the beginning of the event. Following his memory-training courses, hundreds of his students can now perform similar feats. His technique also makes use of visual images and primarily involves the right brain.

To start with, many names actually have immediate visual associations, such as Winter(s), Brooks, Foreman and so on. Lorayne lists 400 in his book, and that list is not exhaustive. Even in these cases the more unusual the image, the better it will be remembered. With a bit of licence, the list of 400 can be greatly enlarged – for example, Fleming might become 'flaming', and Hobson 'hop son', making it quite simple to think of associated images.

So what do you do with these images? Let us start with a hypothetical situation where you need to remember ten names in a particular order. Perhaps you are visiting a large corporation and this is the preferred order for the people you need to see if the first is not in, you ask for the next, and so on. The method is just like that for the story you made up earlier based on a list of random words. Let us say the first name is Stillman. You can visualise a man standing perfectly still – that is all, but you need to see the image clearly – the man might look almost like a tailor's dummy he is so still. The next name might be Livingstone, so you might visualise a living, moving stone. To make the story connection, the still man might be handed a living stone. And the story would go on in this way. You will then be able to recall all the names in the right order just by recalling the story. Why not list ten names from the telephone directory, and see if you can memorise them, in order, using this simple technique? Just to show your mastery of the process, try also reciting the names in reverse order, by running the story backwards in your mind.

With a little imagination, most names can be made into memorable mental pictures, but what of names that have no visual association at all? Let us say, Petrocelli, in which the 'c' is pronounced 'ch'. This name can be broken down, and might become 'pet, roach, L E'. The bizarre picture might thus be you petting a roach, using a letter L and E (the pronunciation of the final I). Or you might make the connection with petrol, and a couple of cellos – 'celli'. A few seconds of thought and a fertile imagination will always produce some visual association, and with practice it becomes very easy. The picturable equivalent does not have to be an exact connection; the name will come to mind even from a very obscure link. This is just where your right brain excels. And having used the image several times, the association will instantly come to mind – the name Howe might be a Red Indian chief saluting and saying 'How', and Campbell might be a big bell being rung to wake some campers.

The same applies to first names. Marion could be linked to marrying, and some wedding image. Keith could be keys; although there is no direct link, the words sound similar enough to make the mental association. If this is not enough, how about a little boy with a lisp holding some keys and saying 'keyth'! Although this might seem like hard work, that one visualisation will suffice for every Keith you ever have to remember.

Having formed a 'picturable equivalent' of a name, how can you link it to a face? Some people readily remember faces, but have difficulty putting a name to them. When meeting a person for the first time, look for any distinctive facial feature. It can be anything that you personally notice immediately – it does not mean the person is abnormal in any way. This feature can be to do with any part of the face – head, ears, and so on. For example, it might be a broad nose. So you might picture, for Miss Brooks, an enormous rubber nose floating down a brook! The sillier the picture is, the easier it will be to recall. The important thing is that it has to have meaning for you, however bizarre. Having made this mental association, you will never be able to look at Miss Brooks again without making the association, and her name will come instantly to mind – even years after you first met. But keep your thoughts to yourself!

Using this technique requires you to be observant, and

this, in itself, will help you to remember names and faces. If all this is too 'right-brain' for you, there are some straightforward tips you can easily follow that will considerably improve your ability to remember names and faces:

1 When you are first introduced, make sure you hear the name, or else ask for it to be repeated.
2 If the name is at all unusual try to spell it. The person will not be offended if you ask them to spell it for you – most people are flattered by your interest.
3 Make a remark about the name, even as simple as 'I once had a colleague called so-and-so.'
4 Use the name during the initial conversation, in a casual, unaffected way – 'That's interesting, Mr so-and-so' or 'Don't you think, George. . .'
5 Use the name when you leave. This reinforces the memory strongly.

Even on their own, these simple rules will improve your recall of names and faces. Adding the visualisation techniques described in this chapter will increase your retention dramatically. Forgetting names and faces need never be a problem again if you use your imaginative right-brain powers in these simple ways.

Once you are aware of the power of pictures you will be able to improve in any area of memory you wish, thinking up your own special methods and devices. If you are not confident enough to commit the main points of a speech or presentation entirely to memory, you can still convert your written notes into picture form. Try converting each subject heading or idea into a single, simple picture. The pictures or symbols need not be properly drawn or detailed, they just need to give you the association you need to expand on a topic, or recall a particular point. At first you will not trust your ability to work in pictures rather than words. But, with practice, you will find there is far more risk of losing your train of thought with a sea of words on several

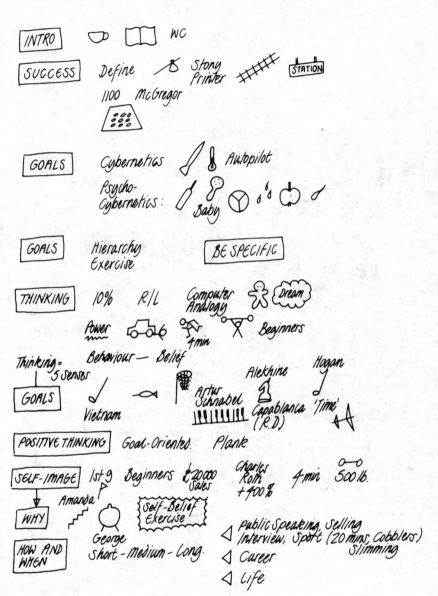

Picture notes for a talk

115

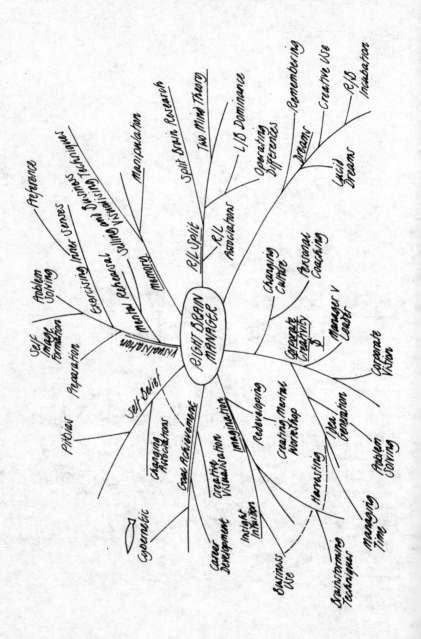

sheets of paper than a few simple picture equivalents.

For a day's seminar, I typically use pictures, symbols, or the odd short word on one side of A4 paper, as the illustration on page 115 shows. Alternatively, I draw these on a single flip chart sheet positioned at the far end of the room, drawn large enough for me to see without turning away from the audience. This eliminates the handling of notes altogether when giving a talk, and is very effective as a memory aid.

Other simple techniques, not necessarily involving pictures, can help creativity, or provide a system for note-taking. For example, you can write the subject title in the centre of the page, then add lines as spokes from the central hub to represent sub-topics, identifying them with one or two words as in the example opposite. Further sub-headings can then be shown as branches from the main spokes, so building up a comprehensive 'thought picture' of the subject on a single page. This is useful when you want to generate lots of ideas, as you can go back to the spokes to extend them, or add new ones as they occur to you, while maintaining the relationship with the central subject. In note-taking you can build up a structure as you listen. This will allow you to create more overall meaning than simply listing the points in the order given.

You can also use this technique as a guide to giving a speech or presentation – it has the advantage that you do not need several pages, with the risk of losing your place. Only the key points are used, and you can add simple pictures to help your recall further.

These simple memory techniques can be applied whenever you need them and will immediately improve your efficiency as a manager. When you use them in conjunction with other creative, 'lateral' ways of thinking there will be no limit to what you can achieve. As we will find in the next chapter, the other crucial factor in the equation is self-image. You need to start *seeing yourself* as a person with a powerful memory and then you will become one.

8

THE SELF-IMAGE THERMOSTAT

WHETHER you are conscious of your self-image or not, it is there, controlling or influencing every part of your life. The self-image is 'the sort of person I am'. It is how you and I see ourselves. It is the sum total of what we believe about ourselves, our attitudes and values. It is a state of mind, and it is reflected in the things we say and do. A healthy self-image, or self-esteem as it is often termed, means having a sense of your inherent worth as a person. It goes with an attitude that says 'I can', or 'I am'. It means self-confidence, self-worth and self-respect. It involves respecting others too, but it primarily means being at peace with yourself. It involves taking responsibility for your desires, thoughts, abilities and feelings – accepting your strengths and acting accordingly. It is complex, because you and I are complex, but as a concept it can be kept simple – it is *how you see yourself*.

For a manager, in a position of leadership and influence, it is something you need to be aware of and be ready to change.

Your self-image affects everything you do. For everyone you come into contact with, it is 'the real you'. It is the blueprint towards which all your physical and mental powers are, maybe unconsciously, directed. Feeling good about yourself – and that is what a positive self-image means – is not an optional extra but a necessity if you want to achieve your personal and professional goals.

High achievers in various fields are aware of the importance of their self-image – and of the role of imagination in creating and upgrading this part of their personality. They understand, though they may express it in different ways, that their self-image controls their life. In other words, if you cannot *see yourself* being a successful person, then you will not succeed. Put simply, you cannot live a lie.

Self-image is dynamic – it can change inexplicably, for better or worse – although it tends to be a longer-term, ever-evolving aspect of your personality, with many of its origins in childhood. At times conscious and at other times unconscious, it is a continual measuring of oneself against the impossible, elusive yardsticks of acquired beliefs about peers, circumstances and the world. But it *can be changed*, by the same creative right-brain imagery you have already used to change specific behaviour patterns and feelings.

However, you cannot treat self-image as you would a specific situation or event you want to be mentally prepared for. Because it is made up of beliefs, it can only be changed by replacing them with new beliefs. You need to see yourself in the desired new role; and such an image will only be strong and clear if you are ready to change any negative beliefs about yourself.

The first step is to gain an understanding of what self-image is all about, and its all-pervading effects on your life. You then need to recognise the personal beliefs on which your self-image is based, acknowledge their irrationality, and be willing to change them. Finally you need to apply visualisation techniques in order to make the required changes to your self-image.

The power of your self-image

The late Dr Maxwell Maltz did much research on self-image. As a plastic surgeon he witnessed at first hand major personality changes in his patients following surgery, which was to be expected as their actual appearance – their outward image – was being changed. However, he was mystified by cases where a low self-image persisted, despite successful surgery, and the removal of the apparent cause of abnormally low self-worth. He would hear pathetic comments such as 'The scar may not show, but it's still there.' A low self-image could persist despite radical cosmetic surgery, and contrary to all the visible evidence. Clearly these patients had deep-seated beliefs that no external change could affect. So Maltz started treating their *emotional* scars, using some of the visualising techniques you have already met.

He cites one man who was so afraid of strangers that he seldom ventured out of his house, yet after using positive visualisation he was able to make his living as a public speaker. Then there was the salesman who was ready to resign because he was 'just not cut out for selling', and six months later was top performer out of a hundred salesmen. Whole business fortunes were turned round. In each case no physical surgery was needed. Only a change in these individuals' beliefs about themselves could bring about the needed change in behaviour.

But a news release by Associated Press a number of years ago cannot be topped for illustrating the sheer power of self-belief. Under the headline 'Just Imagine You're Sane' the article ran:

San Francisco. Some mental patients can improve their lot and perhaps shorten their stay in hospitals just by imagining they are normal, two psychologists with the Veterans Administration at Los Angeles reported.

Dr Harry M. Grayson and Dr Leonard B. Olinger told the American Psychological Association they tried the idea on forty-five men hospitalised as neuropsychiatrics.

The patients first were given the usual personality test. Then they were asked flatly to take the test a second time and answer the questions as they would if they were 'a typical, well-adjusted person on the outside.'

Three-fourths of them turned in improved test performances and some of the changes for the better were dramatic, the psychologists reported.

It is rare for a person to think of him or herself as a complete loser, or conversely as the very personification of human excellence. You may have a high self-image as a manager, but see yourself as lacking in some social settings. More likely, you will have a *range* of beliefs – both positive and negative – that will affect your approach to management. For example, you might see yourself as very effective in interpersonal relationships, yet rate yourself very low on analytical skills, time management, or some other aspect of your work as a manager.

Self-image is clearly a complex phenomenon. It might well embrace all your beliefs, feelings, fears and emotional responses to each and every personal experience up to the present. Its influence is all-pervading, but even making changes in a few specific areas will add much to your overall self-esteem.

Like any skill or activity that has become habitual, the self-image is housed in the subconscious or automatic level of thinking. Your perception of reality is filtered through the lens of your self-image. What you *imagine* to be real, through frequent repetition, becomes your version of reality. High achievers imagine and fantasise about the person they would most like to become – the self-image reads the script, memorises it, and acts accordingly. It operates in line with your beliefs.

Stop comparing yourself with others

You and I can never come out on top if we measure ourselves against others. The odds are against it by at least a few billion! If we persist in doing so, we will end up feeling second-rate and inadequate. The 'logical' conclusion will be 'I'm not worthy,' 'I do not deserve success and happiness.'

Most of us feel inferior at some time in our lives. Few get to be the very best in a career or hobby. Even an Olympic gold medallist will be deficient in activities outside his or her chosen sport. Indeed, the great majority of people have their lives blighted to some degree by *feelings* of inferiority. Note my emphasis on the word 'feelings'. There is no harm at all in accepting objectively that you are not the best. If you are a pianist you will know what it is like to walk away from a live piano concerto, having been spellbound by a virtuoso performance. How do you rank yourself on such occasions? But such an experience need not induce feelings of inferiority. Your self-esteem as a musician can stay intact.

These feelings of inferiority do not result from facts, but from our evaluations of our experiences, our personal perceptions – or beliefs. And these perceptions may have no rational basis whatsoever. Yet we treat them as immutable facts and allow them to control our lives. *Knowledge* of inferior performance need not affect our sense of self-worth or hamper our behaviour. *Feelings* of inferiority most certainly will. 'I failed' may well be a fact. 'I am a failure' is simply a belief without any sound basis.

The self-propelling self-image

Man is programmed by nature to achieve self-set goals; to succeed rather than fail; to overcome any obstacle or problem that presents itself. Thus, the way you see yourself, becomes your internal goal. And natural, goal-seeking mechanisms in your physiology and central nervous system ensure that the goal is reached. This tendency is fundamental to all personal effectiveness, and it is studied in a branch of science known as 'cybernetics', the science of goal-achieving mechanisms.

The original root meaning of the word 'cybernetic' is 'steersman'. A cybernetic system operates by receiving continual feedback on its position so that it can self-correct and thus reach its target. A guided missile is a good example of such a system. The target is well defined, and the many external factors that might throw the missile off course are fed back to the system which then adjusts its trajectory in order to get back on course. As the missile nears its target, the errors become progressively smaller, and the goal is eventually reached. Every part of the system is designed to achieve a single, very clear goal.

An example nearer home is a domestic heating system. You set the goal – a desired room temperature, which is fed into the system. External factors affecting this outcome are monitored – in this case room temperature – and corrections are made by means of an internal power source, the boiler. The targeted temperature is thus continuously achieved.

From what we have seen so far it is no surprise to learn that the human brain, central nervous system and muscular system together comprise a staggeringly complex and efficient cybernetic mechanism designed to achieve its own goals. You have an inbuilt 'personal steersman', to guide you through any obstacles towards the goals you set. You are made to succeed. Your self-image is the internal goal you are relentlessly steered towards. It determines what directions you take, and what you will achieve.

In some cases the cybernetic mechanism works entirely subconsciously. Your pulse and breathing rate are controlled in this way, as are all vital body functions. Although you do not pay them much attention, your body makes constant adjustments to maintain your health. If you are cold, for example, you shiver to generate the necessary heat to correct your temperature. If you get too hot, the same inbuilt wizardry makes you sweat to get your temperature back down to its pre-set 'target' level. Fortunately for all of us, these vital physiological adjustments do not require conscious thought. In fact if you try to take conscious control – for example by thinking about your breathing rate – you will not achieve the optimal natural rate. However, the same cybernetic system can be used, harnessed if you like, to achieve any goals you consciously decide on.

This mind and body partnership, studied in the science of 'psycho-cybernetics', can achieve remarkable goals or 'outcomes.' In this context, great emphasis is placed on *setting goals* – long a foundation of good management and personal effectiveness. More than this, psycho-cybernetics treats the goal as more than a written-down desire or resolution, but the ultimate picture you have of yourself – your self-image.

The phenomenon of striving for goals is both natural and universal; it can be seen from the earliest age. A little child starts noticing bright, moving objects. Her hand reaches out, missing widely, swinging from side to side with little apparent coordination. But gradually the corrections become smaller, and eventually the rattle is held. From then on it is easy. 'Muscle memory' ensures that future goals of the same kind are easily achieved.

The child's conscious mind is then free to concentrate on more important tasks. Having learned to eat with a spoon, her conscious brain can now think about graver matters, such as whether or not she likes rice pudding in the first place. From that point the conscious mind only has to decide to do something, and the automatic pilot takes over. The instructions are stored as permanent chemical changes in the very fabric of the brain, to be recalled and played out at will. You fill your spoon and leave the rest to the cerebellum. Almost all your activities, from getting dressed in the morning to driving your car, are relegated to this automatic thinking mode. But you have to learn to *trust* this amazing inbuilt mechanism. You have to learn to succeed without trying, so that you can think about *where you want to go* rather than *how to get there*.

It is remarkable how behaviour always follows a belief, however illogical or ridiculous it is. A schoolgirl who feels that nobody likes her will find, sure enough, that she is avoided at school social functions. By her total manner – her expression, her self-consciousness or over-anxious attempts to please – she invites rejection. And the actual rejection further reinforces her low self-esteem.

I well recall a teenage family friend blasting his self-written songs through a microphone for hours on end – obviously unaware of the pain his cacophony inflicted on our household and the immediate community. How staggered I was to listen to a professionally recorded cassette tape by the same young man some years later, on which the music and lyrics were by any standards first class. Somehow his belief in his own talent had overcome what sounded, to any discriminating ear, like a hopeless case. His self-image inner goal had become reality.

Recognising your own self-image

Self-image can be conscious or unconscious. Friends and relatives can usually detect the signals of your self-image, but you often can't see the 'house' from the inside. So correcting self-image, is to do with *knowing yourself*, recognising the tell-tale signs, and seeing through the lies and irrational beliefs.

One excellent way of gaining a different perspective on your self-image is through an exercise called non-dominant hand writing. Remember that physically each side of your body is controlled by the opposite side of the brain, so for a right-handed person, when using the weaker left hand, the right side of the brain is used – and vice versa. Where purely physical functions are involved this reversed brain control is not significant, but in the case of writing with the non-dominant hand – that is, using language with the non-language side – some interesting insights can be gained.

Begin by thinking of words that describe you – single words such as 'honest', 'impatient', 'ambitious' etc. With your usual writing hand, write down all the words that come to mind. Put this list to one side, and carry on reading or doing something else. After a while, do another list, but this time using your non-dominant hand. You will no doubt be slow and the words will be hardly legible, but persevere. Just write whatever comes into your mind until you can think of nothing more. Then compare the two lists. This second list can sometimes bring surprises, as the non-dominant list is influenced by the side of your brain that you are less familiar with, and might throw up characteristics that you are not conscious of.

A manager at one seminar found himself describing himself as ambitious. Not only was this term altogether missing from his first list, but he insisted he would never have thought of himself in this way – it just came out in his semi-legible, left-hand scrawl! His close colleagues, however, agreed with the surprising right-brain description. In other cases some of the words on the two lists were in disagreement, as if different people were being described. You can use non-dominant writing whenever you want to get another perspective. By doing this the familiar patterns of the left brain are broken, and you enter a state of mind that is more open to deeper truths about yourself. It is to these self-beliefs that you can then apply visualisation techniques to bring about change.

The first step is to define a positive self-image. Having a positive self-image means:

- knowing yourself, and accepting what you find
- believing in your inherent worth, regardless of the situation
- seeing your position in the world realistically, but with optimism for the future
- having the capacity to recognise your weaknesses and a willingness to change for the better
- recognising your uniqueness, and taking pride in the things that make you unique
- having a healthy admiration for your own abilities, and a positive outlook on what you can achieve
- being willing to try something new, not fearing failure
- having the courage to take your life in your hands and do with it whatever you want to do.

A simple check list will help you recognise your own self-image, and where there is a need for change. Tick any of the following statements which apply to you:

    ☐ I am an optimistic person.

    ☐ I am leading a satisfying, balanced life.

    ☐ I am an enthusiastic person.

    ☐ I project a positive self-image.

    ☐ I am comfortable in new social situations.

    ☑ I look for the good in others.

    ☑ I appreciate and accept sincere compliments.

☐ I use eye contact in conversation.

☐ I am a goal-oriented person.

☐ I don't mind having to make decisions.

☐ I look after my body, and feel it is important to dress well.

☐ I can express my feelings directly.

☐ I can laugh at my own shortcomings and mistakes.

☐ I am able to ask for help without feeling guilty.

☐ I feel comfortable speaking in front of others.

☐ I find that obstacles are a challenge.

☐ I am a good listener.

☐ I accept responsibility for all my thoughts and actions.

A high score indicates a healthy self-image. It shows that you see yourself in a positive, resourceful way. This picture of yourself is the 'thermostat setting' that regulates all your behaviour.

We each have this inner picture of ourselves, as clear and detailed as it is unique. Even though we may find it difficult to describe, and it may not even figure in our conscious thinking, it can be readily observed in all our words and behaviour.

These days it is not easy to reach adulthood with a high sense of self-worth. Parental and educational conditioning, albeit unintentionally, are usually limiting and constraining. Criticism, and pressure to conform, do not produce the uniqueness, individuality and sense of infinite worth that each of us should enjoy, and that are part of healthy self-esteem. Identifying our own self-beliefs is the first step to successful change.

Self-beliefs that rob you of success

The many and varied images you have of yourself can, of course, be positive or negative. That is, they can either be beneficial to you in achieving what you want, or they can be limiting or debilitating. They can be *empowering*, or *disempowering*. You might see yourself, for example, as a naturally outgoing, sociable person, and this is likely to enhance your managerial effectiveness in all sorts of ways as your *actual* behaviour conforms to this positive, healthy image. Similarly, you might see yourself as being good with numbers – an empowering quality for any manager responsible for budgets and cost control. Your *actual* numeracy skills will then be better and your business life will benefit accordingly. Likewise, a negative self-belief – maybe 'I am very disorganised' or 'I am never on time' – will result in negative actual outcomes, hampering your effectiveness as a manager.

These positive and negative self-beliefs control every aspect of your behaviour, even though you may be unaware of them. It is a good idea to list those beliefs that you know apply to you personally – the sort of things you repeat inwardly to yourself without even noticing. Positive self-beliefs, although important, are best left to continue their empowering upward spiral on their own. It is the negative ones that need to be spotted, then squarely faced for change. How often have you heard these sort of expressions?

I can't draw a straight line.
I'm tone deaf.
I couldn't make a speech if you paid me.
I'm hopeless at remembering names.
My mind just goes blank.
I look older than I am.
I can't stand my accent.
I'm a slow reader.

I'm no good with anything mechanical.
People usually take what I say the wrong way.
I suppose I'm stubborn like my father.
I'm always running late.
I'm not really a healthy person.

I suggest you do your own lists – one positive and one negative. This will help you to be more objective and get to know yourself better. It might also help you to spot which beliefs are sensible, and which are quite irrational; which are empowering, helping you to achieve your goals, and which are disempowering, blocking you from accomplishing what you would otherwise be well able to achieve.

A clear understanding of your own self-beliefs is the vital first step to understanding yourself and embarking on the necessary changes to live up to your true potential. And in order to understand your self-beliefs, you need to look at how they originated.

The origins of self-beliefs

Most of your self-beliefs have been formed, unconsciously, from past experiences, successes and failures, triumphs and humiliations, and relationships with other people. Many such beliefs date back to very early childhood, and are deeply etched on your personality, through a lifetime of reinforcement.

If you see yourself, for example, as 'not having a mathematical mind', all your behaviour will conform to this personal perception. Events that contradict this image – such as a high mark in a maths test for someone who is 'no good with numbers' – will be explained away, often ingeniously. The human mind resists incongruence and searches for harmony, so thoughts and actions gravitate towards each other. There is great comfort in being able to say 'I told you so . . . I was right all along. It was just a fluke.'

130

Ask yourself how many of the negative self-beliefs you listed are unchangeable – perhaps due to a genetic defect? Possibly a few; probably none. Can you trace their origins? Is there a logical, factual reason for every belief you now hold about yourself? In most cases, probably not.Let us take as an example Mandy, a professional woman, well liked and quite successful in her career.

Let us turn the clock back some thirty-five years – an easy feat for the human mind. Mandy is playing on the stairs. She overhears her mother chatting with a neighbour in the lounge: 'But Benjamin is the bright one. . .' Benjamin is her older brother. In that moment on the stairs a little seed is sown in Mandy's fertile mind. A few days later she gets something wrong at school. The following week somebody calls her 'stupid'. Two or three random failures reinforce a message that is being etched on Mandy's young mind. Her parents innocently voice some concern. A pattern is being formed.

Soon it appears that she does indeed have trouble keeping up with her school work – but at least there is a 'reason' that little Mandy can understand. She is not very bright – not like her brother Benjamin. To this day Mandy will readily confess, 'I'm not the academic type, I'm a bit slow when it comes to learning.' This clear, self-image governs a large part of Mandy's life, unconsciously, powerfully. And it all dates back to a misguided, chance remark; a single fateful moment in the vulnerable years of childhood. The chance word or event might equally have resulted in a positive, upward spiral of self-esteem. But either way, the young mind was not able to discriminate between truth and a lie.

The origins of our self-doubt can usually be traced to early childhood. But so can the positive beliefs, the dreams, held by so many apparently successful people. Conrad Hilton, of Hilton Hotels fame, would 'play at hotels' as a child. Napoleon 'practised' soldering for many years before

131

he ever went on to an actual battle field. In his 400 pages of notes, he says he imagined himself to be a commander, and '. . . drew maps of Corsica showing where he would place various defences, making calculations with mathematical precision.'

But most of our early conditioning tends to be negative. A delegate I met at a recent conference could pinpoint the very moment when a childhood dream had been shattered. He remembered vividly the place where the car turned, and his uncle's words – 'There's no future for you in rugby. You don't have it in you.' He was able to recall the point at which his whole self-image as someone who enjoyed sport was destroyed, and he understandably felt some resentment. The only unusual aspect of this story is that he was able to remember the exact origin of the negative self-belief and was conscious of its sheer irrationality. Most of us are not aware of the nature and extent of our dominating self-beliefs, values and attitudes – let alone their precise genesis.

Never underestimate the power of an early belief. As a young child I was taught by my older sister to play the piano on a cardboard mock-up of a keyboard, never having experienced the real thing. I could play anything. I never played a wrong note! When, one memorable day, a real shining piano was delivered, I proceeded to play all the tunes on the real piano just as I had on the well-worn cardboard. For months I was obliged to demonstrate my prodigious repertoire to amazed in-laws and neighbours, and I have continued to play by ear to this day.

The first point to note was that I *believed* I could play the piano. And why not? I had been doing it on cardboard for months. My personal self-image thermostat as a pianist was somewhere at the Beethoven or Liszt level! But more than this, for those long hours, I had been *practising success rather than failure*. I had no record of failure to pull me down mentally. Thus, my actual performance was drawn towards a very high self-belief – as with any successful artist, entrepreneur, manager or sports star. Actual mistakes, of which there were plenty when a real piano was tried, were perceived as abnormal ('That's not like me'), and success as normal ('That's more like me'). These are the signs of a healthy self-image. 'I failed' does not mean 'I am a failure'. When psychological barriers are removed, an upward spiral of learning and success is bound to follow. So accept that the origins of your negative self-beliefs are likely to be irrational. And whether irrational or not, they *can* be changed.

The self-image comfort zone

When operating at or close to your self-image, you feel *comfortable*. Behaviour tends towards self-belief, be it positive or negative. And the cybernetic tendency to move towards this comfort zone can be remarkably powerful.

The late Prescott Lecky, a pioneer of self-image psychology, conducted numerous experiments in this field. He saw the human personality as a 'system of ideas', all of which must *seem to be* consistent with each other. Any idea not consistent with the system is rejected – not believed. Ideas that seem to be consistent, or congruent, are accepted. At the centre of all this is the person's self-image.

Lecky was a school teacher and was thus able to conduct experiments involving thousands of schoolchildren. His theory was that if a child had trouble learning a particular subject it was because, from the child's point of view, it was inconsistent for him or her to learn it. By addressing the student's self-conception, he was able to change the child's attitude to the subject. Remarkable successes were recorded. A girl who had repeatedly failed Latin scored 84 per cent. A boy who was said to have no aptitude for English won, the following year, a literary prize. Another student who misspelled fifty-five words out of a hundred and failed in several subjects became one of the best spellers in the school and averaged 91 per cent across the curriculum.

And we can also see this in business situations. Take the case of the '£20,000 a year salesman'. He knows his level within the company sales force, and does his job well – earning, with commission, £20,000 a year. Near the end of one commission accounting year, having already reached the £20,000 mark, he falls strangely ill, and is unable to work for two or three weeks. His doctor can find nothing wrong. Then, just as mysteriously, he recovers at the start of the new commission year and gets back into his comfortable routine of selling. By the twelfth month of that year, however, he is way down on his usual sales quota, with an apparently impossible job to achieve his usual £20,000. Then, somehow, superhumanly, he achieves record sales in the final month, finishing very close to his £20,000 target.

This is a classic illustration of the power of a personal 'thermostat', a comfort zone of performance that is congruent with self-image in any field. Much as under hypnosis, belief completely overrides the reality of the situation, and the whole functioning of the body is affected. Performance and behaviour are drawn towards the level at which you *see yourself*: perhaps the level you feel you deserve; the level you believe you can attain. So if you are below your personal thermostat level, performance improves, and if you are running above, output falls to the level at which you would normally place yourself.

This is where an understanding of self-image can produce truly amazing results. A salesperson who sees herself as a *£100,000* a year salesperson will naturally, relentlessly, cybernetically, usually unconsciously, gravitate towards that higher personal thermostat setting. The only change needed is in what you believe – what you do naturally follows. You do not need to worry about technique and method, cajoling and willing yourself on to success. You simply need to *believe*. So why short-change yourself with limiting, irrational, negative images of your worth and ability? What we usually define as will or persistence, confidence, or even luck – being responsive to random opportunities – is in fact automatic steering towards a self-set goal. It is the power of a dream, a purpose – and it seems to happen without you even trying. This is the mark of personal excellence, the poise and confidence that comes from believing you will achieve what you set out to. Professionalism and training, discipline and willpower will only take you as far as your self-belief allows. You operate within your personal comfort zone. To change it, you have to change your self-image.

Self-image at work in managers

Self-image is not confined to one compartment of your life. Most people tend to amass negative self-beliefs – perhaps in social or domestic areas of life – which can easily spill over into their professional behaviour.

Take, for example, the great psychological divide between the number one and number two positions in an organisation or department. Technically, there is so little difference between the two jobs, but how many managers will blank out irrationally when their mental alarm bells signal that they have stumbled into the wrong league? Or what of the common management task of giving a business presentation? Just how different is giving a presentation in the board room rather than in your own office? For some it can be worlds apart. The question becomes, not 'Am I able to do this?' but 'Is this me: is what I am doing consistent with how I see myself?' The answer, of course, is to see yourself as you want to be. You don't need to kid yourself that you are somebody different, against all past evidence. You simply need to do the visualisation exercises as previously described. And avoid repeating, either outwardly or inwardly, negative statements such as 'I'm no good in front of a crowd', or 'My mind goes blank if I'm put on the spot', which will obviously run counter to the positive changes you are creating. Once the self-image has been changed, these thoughts from your old subconscious image will disappear by themselves.

I have mentioned public speaking specifically because this has been cited as the number one fear amongst managers. This negative self-belief can affect many aspects of management life, from running a departmental meeting to speaking at a conference or seminar, or just giving an impromptu speech at the Christmas party. It is not something to be dismissed lightly. If 'I'm no good at public speaking' is on your list of negative self-beliefs, sooner or later it will surface as a factor in your effectiveness as a manager.

Another important aspect of management is leadership. Unlike specific physical, social or technical skills, it is difficult to train someone to be a leader. This is something that can only be changed through self-belief, using the same visualisation process. In this and other cases involving other people you have to *see the people following you*. Do not be concerned if your imagery has to include people you doubt will ever change their attitude towards you. Including them only adds to the reality of the subjective experience. In time it is you, of course, who will change in many areas – including the way you relate to others. And this is what brings about the overall change in your circumstances and future.

One manager I met had known at the age of fifteen that he would be the manager of a factory. This was a dream, if you like, and he perhaps modelled himself on somebody he knew or knew of. In self-belief terms it was *how he saw himself* in a few years time. Sure enough, by the tender age of twenty-one, he was managing his first plant. And now, true to the upward spiral of his positive belief, he is managing several large plants as part of an overall chief executive function.

Barbara Jacques, a successful writer in the field of dieting, personal appearance and image, runs her own international companies, and speaks to large audiences around the world. Having met her, my lasting impression was of an infectious vitality – and of a pensioner who looked some twenty years younger than she should have looked. But her earlier situation makes all this even more remarkable. For about the first forty years of her life she was a semi-invalid, with all manner of restricting illnesses. The very idea of her speaking to more than a handful of close friends, or writing a book, let alone accomplishing anything of lasting value, would have been ludicrous. She then attended a seminar at which some of the creative visualisation techniques we are describing were introduced, and, after a gap of a couple of years, started to use them. The result was an almost unbelievable change in her life, as each negative self-belief was removed. Without the usual credentials, she embarked on new careers, and literally became the person she dreamed she could be. This was not the result of training, willpower or luck, but of applying right-brain visualisation methods.

Self-image is what makes the difference in business and management. There is more to leading and influencing others than building up knowledge and a range of behaviourial skills. Excellence starts with the way you think. So how do you start putting all this into practice?

Sadly, experience has shown that any amount of positive thinking and affirmation ('I will get that job', 'I will give up that habit'), will not bring a *lasting* change of behaviour unless it is consistent with self-image. This can be most frustrating, as you may sincerely, consciously, believe your positive statements, but remain unaware of the powerful, controlling self-image – the deeper belief – in that area of your life. Further failure, despite following all the positive thinking rules, just reconfirms a failure mode and reinforces a downward behaviour spiral.

What we term positive thinking tends to focus on outward circumstances, problems, obstacles to overcome, and interpersonal relationships. But the real you, what you *are* rather than what you do or say, may remain unchanged and even unrecognised. Affirmations or positive statements might simply *not be believed* by your inner self. Why should they be if they do not fit a well-established track record? After all, what are a few statements compared with a lifetime of self-fulfilling belief? Positive thinking may not be enough. Something more fundamental is involved.

Making the changes

As before, the techniques for making the changes are based on seeing things in the mind subjectively before they happen in the objective world. So all the visualising practice you got earlier will help you achieve the clear imagery you need to make fundamental changes to your self-image.

There is one main difference in the technique for correcting a negative self-image, as compared with preparing mentally for a specific event, such as an interview. To improve your self-image, you need to concentrate more on imagining what it will be like to be the person you want to *be*, rather than the things you think you need to *do* in order to become that person. If you focus on interim behaviour, the existing image will still hold more truth than the conflicting images of new behaviour.

Breaking habits

When visualising, assume that the many changes have taken place, and imagine what it will feel like, and the natural behaviour that will result from being the new person. A lady wrote to me after a personal effectiveness seminar thanking me for the way she had been helped to give up heavy smoking after twelve years. This is how she did it, by applying the general advice given above to her particular situation. She imagined herself over the coming Christmas period as a non-smoker. In her visualisation, she had already broken the habit, and saw herself enjoying different family and social events over the holiday as a different, non-smoking person. She relished the compliments she received for her success, and was flattered to be asked for help and advice by those still locked into the habit. She carried out the visualisation frequently and vividly, developing and clarifying the picture over the weeks. She included as many inner senses as possible, and watched out for the details that make these images so real and powerful. The actual change in behaviour between then and Christmas was a non-event – there was no big issue, no painful transition or repeated attempts to kick the habit. The new person simply 'took up residence' and the old one no longer fitted. And Christmas became what she had imagined it to be as far as the new person was concerned. Emphasising the goal, the result, rather than the way to achieve it, was the secret. It was also important to be able to focus on the Christmas period when she had lots of scope for visualising the new feelings and experiences of the person she was creating inside.

Social gatherings

A manager at a recent seminar described what I have found to be a common negative self-belief. He was unable to relax

at large social gatherings. In particular he had great difficulty entering a room full of people and joining in the
general conversation or approaching an existing group.
This was a major obstacle to his management role, and
something he had tried unsuccessfully to overcome. My
advice to him, mainly in the form of questions, was based on
the same principles. What would it feel like to be a naturally
outgoing person, relaxed at any sort of social event,
whether formal or informal? Can you imagine what it
would feel like – look like and sound like – to be the centre
of attention? What would it be like to be just yourself, and
not make comparisons and self-judgements? To apply this
yourself, choose events that you can picture in detail. Ideally, you should choose a recurring event, which will easily
enable you to imagine the room layout, typical sounds and
other aspects of the whole experience.

This same visualisation process can be applied in any
negative self-image condition. You simply need the imagination to put yourself in the new setting as the new person.
Do not wrestle with *belief* – trying to make yourself believe
that what you want to happen will happen. Repeated imagery *creates* the belief, which is later reinforced as actual
behaviour changes. And you do not need to make your
visualisations in small, timid, 'believable' stages. As you can
imagine *anything*, you may as well go the whole hog and be
whatever you want to be. Why not be the life and soul of the
party!

When looking for chances to put your techniques to the
test, however, you need not give yourself unnecessary hur-
dles. Your next social occasion might be a low-key one
involving mainly close friends, or extended family. And try
not to be in a hurry. The transformation might be instant
and dramatic, or it might take a bit longer. The important
thing is that you will from now always move, cybernetically,
to your new self-fixed, visualised goal. Just keep refining

and repeating the visualised goal – the new person you have already become inside.

Fears and phobias

Another senior manager told me privately about his fear of flying. The nature of his work meant that this phobia – simply an extreme negative self-belief – could easily have jeopardised his career. The same principles described earlier could be applied, but, in the case of phobias, or in-grained habits you wish to change, there are some additional techniques which are remarkably effective, and often bring about instant changes.

First of all think about the phobia, and visualise what happens, based on actual experience. Work round the main representation systems – sights, sounds, feelings, and in this case smells such as the aviation fuel – until you can re-live the experience, although it might be painful to do so. This is an important stage, enabling you to recapture (in this case) the overall feeling associated with flying, but in a deliberate, objective way, for the purpose of understanding and changing it. Apart from this objectivity in the way you are using your natural imagination, your feelings will be quite similar to the anxiety you might go through in the days before a trip, that induce the fear long before you are at the airport. But now you will be thinking about what is happening inside.

Having recalled the experience, you should then identify each of the submodalities at work. In the case of sight, are you seen from outside, or are you seeing as if through your own eyes – is the image associated or dissociated? Is there any part you particularly focused on? How far are you from the sound? Use the checklist in Chapter 3 to remind yourself of the many possible ways of understanding your own particular representation of the experience.

Now recall an experience that is as pleasurable as the flying is painful. Choose some specific memorable event, occasion or experience that you can readily bring to mind in detail. Then go through the same process, clearly imagining the scene, and identifying the different submodalities. What you will then notice is how the submodalities *differ* between the pleasurable and the painful experience, and it is these differences that are important. This is where you do the creative job. Apply the pleasurable submodalities to the unpleasant flying experience. If one image was associated, and the other dissociated, replace the negative (flying submodality) with the positive one. Change the sounds, the focus, the temperature, the size (any characteristics of the whole experience that differ), always putting positive, pleasurable characteristics in place of unpleasant ones. You are then left with a clear visualisation of the phobia experience, but containing all the characteristics that you associate with pleasure. This completely changes the associations, and the overall feeling that the experience brings. The 'phobia' is made up of this mixture of inner senses and feelings. When they are changed, the experience and its associations are changed. When they are removed, the fear is removed.

You can take this a step further, especially in the case of a flying phobia which will usually climax at the same time each time you fly – perhaps when you hear the engines revving up. To do this, you need an independent, objective 'trigger' that will link your pleasurable memory to the unpleasant experience as you are about to undergo it. This can be any trigger you like; you can click your fingers, or make some discreet gesture which is only associated with the pleasant experience you recalled. Each time you recall the positive memory, make the trigger gesture at the most positive, pleasurable moment. Keep to that exact moment each time you mentally rehearse the whole experience. All that remains then is to use the trigger at the critical moment when you are about to fly – thus making an instant association with the full pleasure of the happier memory, and thus enhancing and accurately timing the impact of all the visualisation changes you have made.

You may wish to try this method first on a fairly minor fear rather than a full-blown phobia, just to prove to yourself that you can be flooded with a feeling of happiness when you are not supposed to be. It is not important which technique or combination of techniques you use. What they have in common is the use of right-brain imaginative powers to create the inner reality – to set the cybernetic goal – from which objective experience inevitably follows. Sometimes a less sophisticated use of imagination works just as well.

Leaping over the barriers

You will remember the reframing technique, in which you try to see things from a different perspective. By imagining what it would be like if you were somebody else, or the situation were different, you can usually overcome a mental barrier. This technique can be used in any situation where a low self-image is dragging your performance down. What if you chaired the meeting *as if* you were so and so? What if you gave that presentation *as though* you were a professional speaker, commanding astronomical fees? What if you simply *had* to make a decision immediately – what would your decision be? What if your deadline for that distasteful job was five o'clock this afternoon – not the end of the month? Wouldn't you get it over and done with – and feel much better for it? What would it be like to do those monthly budget figures as if you enjoyed working with figures? Yes, you hate them, but can you imagine what it would be like to enjoy them? Yes you can. There are no limits to your imagination other than those you set yourself. If you can imagine something, you can be it, or achieve it, and feel the way you want to feel about it. The imagining process, the inner visualisation using right-brain thinking, creates the inner goal that you will move towards.

Making this sort of change is sometimes quite scary. This is when you have to leap into the unknown and trust those fathomless right-brain powers; be prepared to discard cherished beliefs; perhaps abandon a familiar prop. But making changes for life, changes that will bring you pleasure and personal success, are worth a few mental leaps. Have a long, honest look at your list of negative self-beliefs, and, one at a time, start creating the changes you decide on.

9

THE PRACTICE OF
SUCCESS

RIGHT-BRAIN THINKING is largely subconscious, so we have little direct control over our intuition, dreams, and the ideas that can sometimes flood our imagination. But there are some positive, constructive ways in which you can use right-brain imagery to bring about specific and tangible results. Often termed 'creative visualisation'. such techniques can be applied in all sorts of ways – from solving problems and making better use of your time as a manager to fulfilling major life goals. This chapter concentrates on some of these practical applications of visualisation.

Being successful is about achieving goals, and your human cybernetic system is designed to steer you along whatever pathways will lead you to those goals. The goal starts out, however, as a clear picture in your mind, the inward experience of some outward reality. But, first, let us see the power of this process of creative visualisation at work.

An American prisoner of war is confined to a tiny cell in Vietnam. Back home he played golf off a handicap of three. (For non-golfers, that means he was very good.) Every day, impervious to his squalid surroundings, he practises mentally a round of golf. First exhausting every course he has ever played on, imagining in every detail the strokes, he relives and then perfects, in mental images, previous games. He then proceeds to 'play' courses that he has only seen on television, and goes on to imagine successful rounds on other famous courses unknown to him.

Shortly after his release and return to the USA he plays in a competition. To the amazement of fellow-golfers and the press, he achieves a score of three over par – the standard he was at before the war. Asked the secret of his success after being out of the game for so long he is a little offended, responding that he never three-putted a green in five and a half years of daily practice in Vietnam!

The effect of so-called 'mental rehearsal' on performance has been well researched. The journal *Research Quarterly* reported an experiment on the effects of mental practice on improving skill in sinking basketball free throws. One group of students actually practised throwing the ball every day for twenty days, and were scored on the first and last days. A second group was similarly scored on the first and last days, but without any practice in between. A third group was scored on the first day, then spent twenty minutes a day *imagining* they were throwing the ball into the net.

The first group, which actually practised for twenty minutes each day, improved their scoring by 24 per cent. The second group, which had no sort of practice, showed no improvement. The third group, which practised in their imagination only, improved their scoring by 23 per cent! Almost identical results were achieved without any physical practice. Similar experiments have been done involving darts and archery, with similar remarkable results.

Such 'mental rehearsal' is familiar to many managers, and can be a natural and instinctive part of their thinking, although they are often not aware of the process they are using. The experience of one manager attending one of our seminars illustrates both the effectiveness of the technique, and how it is often applied instinctively. He was an amateur glider pilot and had a major test coming up in a few days – if I recall correctly, to get his pilot's licence. His big problem was that, after the many flying hours he had undergone, he had yet to carry out a single proper landing, and this was causing trepidation and loss of sleep as the test day approached. On the night before the big event, almost overcome with worry, he could do no more than lie awake in bed, and repeatedly imagine himself performing landings – perfect landings – one after another.

Following his test the next morning he was delighted to receive the congratulations of the examiner for passing. But the examiner's remarks were more significant. Of the many tests he had conducted, of professionals as well as amateurs, the landing he had seen that day was probably the most perfect! A happy manager walked away on air. A first ever perfect landing? No. He had carried out so many the previous night that they had become second nature. He had gained the confidence he needed through visualisation – mental practice – without ever having heard the term or understood the powerful mental technique he had been using. Mentally practised success was translated into reality.

Such techniques have been around for a long time in business, especially in selling.

In his book *How to make $25000 a Year Selling* (more than thirty years of inflation ago) Charles B. Roth tells how a group of salesmen in Detroit tried an idea which increased their sales by 100 per cent. Another group in New York, using the same visualisation techniques, increased sales by 150 per cent and individual salesmen improved their performance by up to 400 per cent. Roth explained how the technique worked:

The reason why it accomplishes so much is that selling is simply a matter of situations. One is created every time you talk to a customer. He says something or asks a question or raises an objection. If you always know how to counter what he says or answer his question or handle the objection, you make sales . . . A role-playing salesman, at night when he is alone, will create these situations. He will imagine the prospect throwing the widest kind of curves at him. Then he will work out the best answer to them . . . No matter what the situation is, you can prepare for it beforehand by means of imagining yourself and your prospect face to face while he is raising objections and creating problems and you are handling them properly.

Roth's salesmen were using the same technique of mental practice, with remarkable results. And this technique can be applied to any business situation where you do not know what you will have to face, and need more confidence.

Two fundamental principles help to account for the success of mental practice. First, the brain *cannot differentiate* between the visualised practice, and the equivalent in the external, objective world. The neural messages are the same, so to all intents and purposes, *actual* experiences are being recorded. Secondly, negative practice is unnecessary – *you do not practise mental failure, just success*. So you can bypass all the failures involved in physical practice. Mental practice has no such obstacles to overcome.

Your own special place

In Chapter 5 I described the way visualising a pleasant scene or place can help you relax. But if you are to practise success in everyday life you will need something rather more than this. A special place, yes. But somewhere where you can transact any kind of subjective business you need to, from solving problems to changing negative self-beliefs. If you like, you need a super office-cum-laboratory-cum-information library so that all the resources you need will be at your disposal.

Everyone needs a special place, some form of retreat or sanctuary, a place that is safe and serene. In real life few of us have a place that is exactly the way we would want it. But you can create such a place in your mind.

If you could have the most wonderful place in the world, in which you could create and work and be productive, where would it be? And what would it be like? Imagine you can have such a place, and start creating it in your mind. It can be wherever you like, in town or country, anywhere in or out of the world. So think carefully about where it will be. No doubt you will want the most beautiful views, or some scene out of the window that gives you particular pleasure. It could be a real place that you visited on holiday, or a place deep in your childhood memories. Or part remembered and part created – you create it as you wish.

Get into your alpha state, using the 3-2-1 method, and start imagining. This can be a most pleasurable experience. You know the excitement of setting up your first home, or completely furnishing a room as you wish, really creating something that is yours. Just imagine your dream place in the same way. Take your time. You don't need to rush – it might become a lifetime refuge and creative workshop, so it is well worth the time. Organise all the furnishings, the things you will want to have at hand, books, tools you may want to work with in your hobby or profession, everything you might need to live a full, creative, productive life. Will you have music? What information might you need? All the information in the world is available to you and can be in your Special Place.

Now make a list of the things you do *not* want to have in this place. These things need never come in. All the things that spoil your pleasure in real life can be banned.

Your personal adviser

In your imagination you can return to this room whenever you wish. Get to know your favourite chair, and where you will sit, and where your books, desk and other things will be. No one can ever visit you without an invitation, but you may wish to have a Special Friend as a regular guest, and this can be a person you actually know or know of, or a purely imagined person. You can consult with this Special Person whenever you wish. He or she will always be available, to give advice, and help you solve any problems.

How do you do this? Visualise the person clearly, and ask them what you wish. Discuss with your Adviser any problems – even if you have no idea what the solution might be. Imagine getting an answer – any answer they happen to give you. If you have difficulty, imagine what they *might* say if they were giving you help and advice. You will gradually become less inhibited about doing this, and will learn to trust the advice you are given. This, of course, is simply a device to harness your own creative insights, but you are more likely to listen to and act on the advice of someone you have great respect and admiration for. You are simply using your right-brain faculties more productively.

Setting up this place is an important step in getting to know your subconscious self. It might fuel long-standing desires, or allow you to be specially creative in whatever way you wish. It may help you reassess your priorities and work out what is really important to you. Note your feelings as you get to know this place, and start using it in your subjective world to accomplish whatever you wish in your objective world.

You have taken a critical creative step. You can enter your Special Place whenever you wish by counting downwards, and going into your alpha state. This is your secret retreat. You will always be safe here. You will always feel happy, whatever is happening in your objective world.

You are now beginning to feel at home in your inner world. You have your Wise Person, and your Special Place. You have equipped yourself to accomplish whatever you wish. You can now begin to practise success on a routine basis.

When to use mental practice

In what situations will this technique be needed? First, when a mental habit (an attitude, feeling, association or belief) is preventing you from achieving your best. Go back over the list of negative self-beliefs you made in Chapter 8. Each of these will need some positive practice in order to make the change part of you.

You can also use this technique when you want to be mentally prepared for difficult or negative situations (such as not being able to answer questions at an interview, a blown overhead projector bulb when giving a presentation, an angry customer creating a scene) or unknown situations as in the case of Charles Roth's salesmen. By practising eventual success even when facing such obstacles, you will have the confidence to be ready for anything that might be thrown at you, however unlikely. In a recent important conference workshop presentation in Brussels, my co-presenter had to battle against the tooting horns of trucks that had gathered immediately outside the hotel for a protest rally. At the same time the projector bulb blew. Apart from a barrage of bruised tomato missiles from the delegates a worse situation could not be imagined. Or could it? If you can vividly imagine then mentally overcome such eventualities, the actual event will lose all its power to terrify.

Then there are some situations where you simply do not get the opportunity to practise, because of the nature of the activity. For instance, you may have to give a broadcast or press interview, or address a large conference. For most managers these events do not happen frequently enough to allow confidence to be built up by actual experience. This category includes the first time you do any demanding activity.

Let me illustrate such a case. I was talked into being the guest speaker on a phone-in programme on a local radio station – on a subject outside my main specialisation. I had done no broadcasting before, and had never been inside a radio studio, but the producer was not aware of this. Despite repeated telephone calls before the date of the broadcast, a minute before the scheduled start time I still had not been briefed or given any idea of what would take place. And it did not seem professional to run screaming out of the building having been politely served a coffee during my long wait. The briefing eventually came during the playing of the first record of the programme, and by then it was too late to worry anyway. Although adrenalin and healthy nervous tension played their part, the only way I could cope with such a new experience was through prior imaginative preparation – mental practice. The more you get to rely on this right-brain process, the more you will accept hitherto daunting or distasteful challenges, and get into the habit of success. You will start living up to your true potential.

Few people get enough opportunities for practice in these sort of areas. Yet such once-in-a-while tasks have to be faced by almost every manager – for example making someone redundant, or disciplining a member of staff. These management tasks may be infrequent but they still have to be carried out effectively and professionally. So you need to create your own practice opportunities. Because of the built-in 100 per cent success rate – you always achieve the outcome you aim for – mental practice is much more effective in any event.

Problem-solving

Solving problems is a large part of any manager's responsibility. Indeed, effectiveness in this area covers just about all there is to management – people problems, communication problems, customer problems and so on. A manager is essentially a problem-solver.

In the chapter on imagination and intuition we saw that a lot of managers found that answers to problems would emerge at odd times, such as when waking in the morning, during a car journey, when shaving or showering, or when day-dreaming. Unfortunately this type of problem-solving occurs in such an unstructured way that you cannot always rely on it happening when required. The best advice is to allow yourself time, and become experienced at relaxing in your Special Place, to allow these answers to come to the surface of your mind, always making sure you have a notebook and pencil at the ready.

The mirror technique

But there are also specific problem-solving techniques that use right-brain powers. One might be called a 'mental mirror'. To use this technique, visualise the problem as if in a large, full-length mirror, and form a clear image that depicts the situation you want to change. By closing your eyes and lifting them upward a little, seeing the mirror a little distance away rather than immediately in front of your eyelids, you should be able to get a clear picture. Then visualise the answer to the problem – what the picture will look like when the problem no longer exists. For instance, if the problem is to do with excessive stock levels, you can visualise a lower level – less physical stock in the warehouse, lower costs and better profits – even though you may not know how the solution will be achieved. If your problem is that your house will not sell, you can visualise the solution – your house with a sold sign outside.

Do this in a relaxed, alpha state, using the 3-2-1 method. You can make the mirror as big as you like to include whatever you want to show the problem clearly. Give the 'problem mirror' a blue frame – and always associate this and any problem with a blue-framed mirror. Now picture the solution in another mirror immediately to the left of the problem mirror. This mirror is framed in white, and whenever you project in your mind a white-framed mirror you are seeing the solution to a problem. Make the image as clear as you can. Use different angles and focus, and incorporate sounds and feelings as well as images. The mirror is like a panorama, opening up a real scene that shows the solution you would like to see. Visualise these two scenes as often as you like from your alpha state, but always switch from the problem mirror to the solution mirror so that a strong association is created – blue frame to white frame, problem to solution. From then on, subconsciously, when you think about the problem, the white-framed solution will appear. And this represents the goal that you will cybernetically move towards. This technique can be applied to any problem at all when you know the solution, but do not know how to achieve it. All that is needed is to see the problem clearly, and also see it overcome. Make sure, incidentally, that you have a place for these mirrors in your Special Place.

If your problem concerns personal relationships – say with a boss, client, or member of your team – you can probably easily visualise the problem situation or situations. But it is vital to go on, to clearly envisage how, ideally, you would like things to be. How will the person look, speak and act? Think of the other benefits of solving this problem – visualise them and enjoy seeing them in your white-framed mirror.

You can also adapt this technique to overcome any negative self-image or habit. See yourself first as you are, in the blue-framed mirror, then see yourself as you want to be – with the problem solved – in the white-framed mirror to the left. In addition, you can use your mirrors for career advancement. Your 'problem' in this case is simply is that you are not now where you want to be – in career terms. Simply decide where you want to be, and picture and savour the whole scene. This becomes your solution mirror image.

What about when you do not know (that is, cannot even imagine) a solution to the problem? In this case go over the problem in your alpha state before going to sleep. See it from different angles, as already described. This not only gets things into perspective when you are in a relaxed, non-emotive state – and this sometimes results in a problem immediately seeming smaller and less troublesome – but forms the 'instruction' to your subconscious to work on the problem. On waking the following morning, get back into your alpha state through the quick 3-2-1 method, and spend a few minutes pondering the matter again. Often during this period answers, new angles, or a line of pertinent questions will emerge. If not, do not force the matter, just try and remain receptive through the day, if possible finding further opportunities to go through the countdown relaxation technique to enter alpha. If you regularly recall your dreams, you may also wish to use the dream control technique for problem-solving described in Chapter 6.

Time management

Problem-solving is one vital aspect of good management; another is being able to manage your time.

Let us start by looking at the size of the problem. An American, Dr De Woot, came up with some dramatic findings concerning corporate executives. He concluded that for all executives with no previous time management training:

- 49 per cent of their time is spent on jobs that their secretaries could do
- 5 per cent of their time is spent on tasks that could be delegated to subordinates (I would have guessed a far higher figure)
- 43 per cent of their time is spent on work that could have been delegated to colleagues

This leaves only 3 per cent! Even a modest improvement would certainly leave plenty of time for the job functions that only you can and should do, as well as ample time for home and leisure, not to mention a bit of creative visualisation in your Special Place. Converted into gross salary and extras, as compared with equivalent secretarial or subordinate costs, De Woot's figures also quickly help to explain company overspending, losses, corporate malaise, and the thousands of bankruptcies and receiverships where the final decision has been finely balanced. This is where real effectiveness begins. And we need the imagination to grasp the opportunity fully.

Those of us who have been on time management courses, and read some books on the subject, can smugly adjust Dr De Woot's figures, which you will note applied to executives who had not undergone any time management training. Sadly, other research into the effectiveness of training programmes generally shows a remarkable loss of retained and applied knowledge, in weeks and months, and certainly within a year. So there is room for improvement on a grand scale, and *ongoing* improvement as we transfer success from one area of weakness to another.

You can begin by changing practices which common sense tells you are robbing you of time. Applying the sort of creative thinking you have already explored, *quantum* changes are there for the making. If you want to prove to yourself otherwise – that no such slack applies to your hectic schedule – you will win the argument easily and find yourself unable to save any time. Belief sets its own rules and wins every time.

Equally, if you have never achieved better than a 10 per cent improvement in the past, goes another common argument, it is surely irrational to expect more. Such sequential thinking lies at the heart of orthodox education and training, of contemporary mental conditioning, and popular time management theory. If, further, you have been schooled in economic laws such as that of diminishing returns, you will be easily convinced of an even lower target – so why even bother trying? These embedded mediocre expectations are totally self-fulfilling, and help to explain the failure of many traditional time management training courses. As soon as the course is over, entrenched attitudes, unrecognised and unexplained, win the day back in the office. We need not fear enemies without, but enemies within. Time is not in the habit of change. The needed change is in us.

Unlearning left-brain time management rules

In what other ways does our historical conditioning affect future performance? One of the established time management rules is to establish realistic goals, and in particular timescales. This is because of our tendency to be over-optimistic in planning how much we can achieve. How many items on the daily or weekly 'to do' list get carried over? So if a job has taken two hours in the past, it is realistic to use this as the time allocation, adding perhaps 10 per cent 'slack' – having decided it is a legitimate job for us to do in the first place. But now just think about this in the right-brain, creative mode you have begun to tap. If that job had to be completed as a final task before going off on a long-awaited holiday, or as a direct assignment from on very high, quite remarkable things might happen. You would somehow achieve the impossible. The ridiculous deadline requires impossibility thinking – lateral, right-brain thinking, all the creativity and insight you can call upon. There may be short cuts you had never thought of, parts you can delegate, corners you can cut without affecting the main outcome. Why are you able to achieve such miracles towards the end of the day to catch the post, or get some urgent task finished? Different mental powers are unleashed when you move out of the rational, familiar, vertical thinking mode. This is the ubiquitous cybernetic model at work, locking tenaciously onto whatever target is programmed in, refusing to believe in impossibility.

Acting 'as if'

The secret is to act 'as if'. What if you *had* to do the job in half the time? What would change? What if you had to do the job in one quarter the time – or if by achieving such you were offered some special reward, promotion or whatever? What if your very job was on the line, as on occasions it may well have been? This courageous thinking is the province of the right brain. It delights in such pretend games. Using the visualisation and imagination techniques already described, you can call on these mental reserves at will. Why do you go to the busy person to be sure the job will get done? Because he or she has learned the secrets of self-management, of handling new and apparently limitless responsibility, of attaining goals by whatever means it takes. So if real circumstances can dramatically increase our outputs – deadlines, clearly defined goals and priorities – right-brain time management skills can be used to 'induce' those mental states.

We have already seen that the brain does not differentiate between real and imagined senses. Nor is there any doubt that you have the childhood skill of imagining whatever you want. So powerful right-brain resources can be called up at will by the simplest mental devices, by asking naive questions when you are paid to give clever answers, by seeing things in a different way, by applying the problem-solving mirror techniques to time problems.

What are you worth?

Most time management books tell you to put a value on your time. This analytical process might be alien to non-financial people, and appear somewhat mercenary. But the underlying principle is about more than dollar and pound signs, it is about thinking about things from another angle – using the lateral right brain. Such a mental device is simple but potent. There are business trips you will not make. There are tasks you will delegate. There are better, quicker ways of doing things. There are final details you will not pursue, arguments you will not get drawn into, people you will avoid, all because you begin to think in terms of your value per hour, per minute. And don't forget the extra costs, the overheads, and the downwards and upwards ripple of inefficient management of your time.

Management effectiveness is very rarely to do with crossing the last 't' and dotting the last 'i'. When detail is important, the question becomes 'what detail?' And this is where the top time managers score – in getting to the core issues and knowing when a detail is significant to the achievement of the overriding goal; where time is best invested. And there is no doubt that bringing apparently minor and unrelated issues to the surface is a right-brain function. The holistic right brain can survey an array of meaningless data, and spot the associations that make sense. It can look at the same set of variables in a different way and throw up new possibilities. This is the paradoxical 'don't try too hard' technique. You need a simple insight rather than further tiers of analysis.

In time management courses, procrastination rightly gets the blame for much lost time. This is rarely due to technical inability to get on with the job, but rather to fear of failure, or success, or some other unexplained mental restraint. It is to do with how you see yourself, with the match or mismatch between what you are and what you do. A negative self-belief is likely to be at the root of habitual procrastination. So visualising yourself as the person you want to be will provide the inner direction needed. Trying to tackle this tendency to put off important decisions or avoid difficult situations through painfully willing yourself to change your behaviour is likely to result in failure and further bouts of guilt. See yourself as you will be, and leave it to your cybernetic subconscious to decide upon the best means to achieve the end you have determined.

Super organisation can block creativity

There is another way in which the right brain refuses to fit into time management orthodoxy. Dr McGee-Cooper, a researcher at Columbia University, has observed traits of high creativity among those who can never seem to get organised – the people who file in piles on their desk and keep everything in sight. These people, she has found, generally showed a right-brain dominance. Such people find traditional time management rules too confining and unstimulating because they need to give their intuition and natural interest a free rein as they work. The harder they try to stick to the rules, the more frustrated and unproductive they become.

Ellen Langer of Harvard University says something similar; that the rigid, automatic thinking promoted in traditional time management theory leads to 'mindlessness' in right-brain dominated people, which, in turn, reduces their productivity. She goes on to say that *mindfulness* is seeing the *novel in the familiar*. The flexible and creative style of right-brain-dominated people turns stumbling blocks to productivity into building blocks, thereby increasing productivity. Mindfulness, she says, alleviates burnout by motivating people to find innovative solutions to the same problems. It seems, then, that for certain people, traditional time management training can be seriously counter-productive.

Intuition, as we have described it, figures very little in traditional time management wisdom. However, the right brain has everything to do with how you decide to spend your time to be more productive. No schedule in the world will make you productive if you really don't want to work. So for such people, the answer to increased productivity is not to become better organised by making lists, prioritising activities and scheduling. It is, rather, to create an atmosphere that motivates that person – and this can be accomplished in a variety of ways with a bit of ingenuity and right-brain thinking.

All work and no play . . .

One key element in higher personal productivity is a sense of fun. To boost productivity, researchers suggest working less and playing more. This is a long way from many time management theories which suggest working through lunch breaks and always carrying work with you in case you are caught waiting for an appointment. Instead, you can relax by reading a book or magazine. Many researchers have also found that exercise can help boost productivity, creating a sense of well-being which alleviates the stress that leads to low productivity. Other theorists recommend different forms of meditation to create a restful level of consciousness, which, again has been found to improve overall output. Ignoring the clock may be the best way to utilise time, as strict schedules are too confining to the right-brain-dominated person, and therefore reduce productivity.

All this fits well with everything we have seen so far about the need for greater recognition and encouragement of our inherent creative faculties. What remains to be seen is whether corporate training professionals and management development budget controllers will begin to incorporate this awareness into existing and planned management training courses.

The right-brain manager need not fear time pressures and the ills they induce. He or she uses the whole mind, for which no problem has yet been found too hard, no obstacle insurmountable. Like the outer cosmos it ponders from time to time, the human mind has no known limits. And the only limit on what you can accomplish in seven days a week is the limit on which you, whether consciously or unconsciously, decide.

Creating your own future

The practice of success involves understanding the particular strengths of the under-utilised right brain and practising the specific techniques described. These principles and techniques can be applied to *every aspect of management and personal life*. They represent a better way of thinking, a better way of living.

We have looked at the application of right-brain thinking to problem-solving, and to better use of time, as two dominant areas of management practice, as well as to imminent events or situations that need to be faced with greater confidence. And the same techniques are as powerful in changing the self-beliefs identified in Chapter 8. With a little imagination you will be able to apply right-brain concepts and techniques to any area of management. I have used problem-solving, time management and leadership as major examples of applications. Planning, for example, will encompass visualising desired outcomes, perhaps with alternative scenarios, as well as written, analytical processes. This is what top managers are able to do well. Decision-making, as we have already seen, can harness intuitive powers far more sophisticated, and indeed reliable, than any analytical technique.

By applying these methods on a regular basis you will experience changes over days, weeks and months, and each success will fuel your confidence in achieving further goals. But you can also apply visualisation to achieve longer-term goals – major career changes, job advancement, or other 'life goals' that, by their nature, might require years rather than weeks to be accomplished. In cybernetic terms, your goal might well involve new beliefs about yourself, but also a particular outcome you desire – a different job, skill, or the fulfilment of an ambition. All the visualisation techniques can be used, but you are now *creating* – in a positive rather than corrective way – *your own future*.

As your personal desires are limitless in scope, constrained only by your imagination, all I can do is give an example that can be modified to apply to your own desired achievement.

Your passport to corporate success

Let us say the goal is to become the managing director of a £100 million company within five years. In a cybernetic sense the time it will take to achieve such a goal may have to be left undecided, affected as it is by the myriad variables that will be fed back into the system. So you may have to use broad time goals – say between three to five years, or between five and seven years, as seems appropriate. If you wish to add some urgency, the visualised goal can to some extent accommodate this, even by the inclusion of specific diary or calendar dates within the visualised goal, or a projected car registration year on the BMW! But do not overstretch the technique by seeing yourself sitting in the Prime Minister's chair reading next Thursday's *Financial Times*!

Let me stress that I need not have chosen a goal involving material success – the goal might have been to get off the business treadmill and achieve an idyllic, rural, self-sufficient existence. Alternatively, the goal could be in the political, sporting or literary arenas, or for that matter a bigger business target – say chairperson of a multi-billion corporation. None of that matters – it is your decision. You simply need to apply the cybernetic, visualising principles and techniques. The only limiting factor is your imagination; if you cannot imagine yourself in the role, it is certain you will not achieve it.

So, first visualise yourself as the MD. Do what you did in the earlier visualisation exercises. Clarify each detailed sensory experience so that you *become* your desired outcome. You will need to feel and smell the leather chair, enjoy the silent carpet underfoot, experience your new boss-like economy of words and actions, the cosseted drive to the office. You become what you want to become, but it starts in your mind. Then, over the coming years, all your physical and mental resources are drawn into the cybernetic feedback loop, steering you to your decided goal.

A left-brain question might be raised in your mind. What happens during the five-year period, apart from the habitual revision and practice of the new person? How does all this work? Well, you instinctively move towards the goal by your behaviour, interests and attitudes because different things now attract your attention; things that somehow have an association with your visualised goal. What happens, for example, when you change your car? Almost every other car on the road seems to be the same model. Another little world has opened up to you because your particular car now has a special place in your mind. So you notice things that are associated with what is now of importance to you. This association is usually subconscious. Some otherwise meaningless words, sounds or images that register when you are driving to work can start you on a train of thought, or give you an idea, that will influence what you then do. The association, the link, is with what was already of interest to you – even deep in your subconscious. And it is this subconscious power of association that 'steers' you over the months and years.

So how does this associative power manifest itself in the transition to managing director? A job advertisement appears after a couple of years that would mean a quantum improvement on your present lot, and hitherto would have been far outside your league. But the job now looks a possibility. Why? Because what you read, or what otherwise reached your conscious mind, fitted well with your new self-image as a successful managing director. Then, with the new-found confidence that your inner image gives (and a bit of specific interviewing visualisation to help you along), the intermediate job is landed; you are moving in the right direction.

While this is happening, you might begin to dress, walk, talk and generally behave differently – more congruently with the new, inner you. Friends and family begin to notice. At the same time any shortcomings in knowledge, skills and experience become more noticeable in the light of the new self-image. So new training pursuits, reading, and other preparation will be inevitable. But this will happen naturally – it will seem the obvious thing to do. And, importantly, you will enjoy doing these things, as they are all associated with a pleasurable inner goal. Time and energy will always tend to be expended on this big goal. One step at a time, interim goals will be achieved. Parts of the dream will become reality. Your attitudes will change. The envisioned goal might be revised or clarified further. Succeeding becomes routine, rather than random.

Two lessons for goal achievers

Having talked to many top managers who have used right-brain visualisation to get them to where they now are, I have learned two particularly valuable lessons about the whole amazing process.

First of all, make sure that you have created and visualised *new goals* before you reach the one you are now moving towards. To reach a major life goal without another, probably far bigger goal well developed, and to which you are already moving, will not give the satisfaction expected. That is, every goal is an *interim* goal; no goal, when reached, will bring with it the ultimate state of mind you are striving for – there will always be new dreams, new perceptions of pleasure and pain. A number of senior managers I met had aspirations either within their present career path and industry, or in completely different areas such as politics, writing, self-employment, or concerning their family life. While still enjoying the *journey* to the next goal, they had formed new goals, new dreams that had begun their incubation long before the current goal had materialised. A visionary without a vision is a broken person. And a vision realised is no longer a vision.

The second major lesson concerns one of the most common questions about long-term goal achievement – how can my personal visualisation take account of all the external factors, including the people on whom I will depend, things right outside my control? First of all, the visualised goal should be an *outcome*, rather than the way that outcome will be reached. If Edinburgh is your goal (to use a simple analogy), you can drive or fly or walk or take the train or be beamed there – you can do it quickly, cheaply, scenically, directly or indirectly. In fact there are infinite combinations of ways in which you can get there, and you may change strategy many times. So do not tie yourself down. *Allow the cybernetic mechanism to choose*, step by step, moment by moment, using the vast resources of your subconscious to make the winning associations. A missile targeted on New York is not programmed to take in the fantastic views of the Grand Canyon en route!

Let me illustrate this. A group managing director, who has very strong right-brain tendencies and is at home with visualised goal achievement, almost had his self-belief shattered as he was almost within reach of a major career goal – in fact another MD position. His mistake was that his goal, and all his practised visualisation, concerned a present boss, on whom his plans depended. This boss was removed from his own position summarily and everything collapsed for the manager. From this manager's experience the rule is obvious; do not put all your eggs in any one basket – particularly the basket of individual people; do not restrict yourself to your present company – it may not exist by the end of your timescale; be cautious about tying yourself down even to an industry, and certainly to a small sector of your industry. There are hundreds of £100 million turnover businesses, plenty of these are in rural environments (so feel free to include your room with a view), they all need managing directors, and for the right person, will offer all the perks you might visualise. And you can easily change the colour of the carpet. So do not build into your visualised goal any constraints that are not *essential* for you to realise that goal.

There are plenty of sound hypotheses as to why and how this visualising process works, even for major life goals. But concentrating on the process rather than where you want to be will actually impede your progress. The unconscious right-brain cybernetic system does not need conscious interference. Trying hard does *not* guarantee success. There has to be a dream. And the dream takes you forward. That is what it means to practise success.

10

CORPORATE MANAGER 2000

COMPANIES do not have ideas; people have ideas. People innovate and get things accomplished, usually *despite* corporate cultures and structures. But most people work in the context of an organisation, whether large or small, so we need to look at how the role of the manager might change in the wake of new ways of thinking, moving towards a new kind of whole brain manager, Manager 2000.

Corporate effectiveness starts with the individual manager. Usually one or a few 'special' people account for remarkable organisational success stories. In most of the largest multinationals it is the power of personal creative thinking, and visionary leadership, rather than some corporate alchemy, published mission statement or quality programme that accounts for the all-pervading culture of success.

Working within your organisation

Will your new impossibility thinking mean that you will outgrow your present organisation? Will a switch to right-brain thinking or a change in self-image mean rethinking your overall career path? Possibly. But the growing interest in the 'intrapreneur' – the entrepreneur operating within a corporate environment – and the success of some companies in harnessing internal creative power means that leaving to set up your own business is only one of the options.

In some cases the exit option would be better both for you and your organisation. Being a square peg in a round hole rarely brings happiness or personal fulfilment. It is more likely to bring regrets and poor health – hardly beneficial to you or your company. And the cybernetic route to your goals might take you in unexpected ways. In other cases, however, your enhanced managerial effectiveness might allow you to make a greater impact inside than out. At first glance this would tend to apply more to senior positions, where greater influence can be exerted. But this need not always be the case. An individual working creatively and using their mind in the ways we have seen is sure to get noticed and eventually rewarded. In addition, many managers are far happier working with other people in a corporate environment. For such people the life of an independent entrepreneur might well be too isolated.

Furthermore, unless you are a corporately owned workaholic with no outside personal interests, then a new way of thinking will probably enrich your social and domestic life – your extra-corporate life – as well. This is the holistic approach to management development, in marked contrast to earlier 'human resources' thinking. Enlightened companies will recognise and develop their managers in this fuller way, and will certainly benefit from their increased creativity.

Personnel management (as it used to be termed) embraces the individual as well as the organisation. So for all the theories about organisation, structure and culture, there are complementary theories addressing the personal aspects in the form of motivational theories. What makes people work harder? What makes people happier in their jobs? In the middle are the 'role' theories, concerning the many different 'hats' we wear. Your role as manager is just one of many – perhaps you are also a mother, for example, from time to time a scapegoat, and probably a neighbour.

These theories based on the individual all have three major shortcomings. Firstly, they aim to understand people better with a view to improving organisational perfor- mance. But such an aim severely limits understanding; people are not *just* corporate resources. Secondly, they have a predominantly *behavioural* perspective. It is easier to watch rats than understand human thinking; so beliefs, attitudes and feelings have been left outside the accepted boundaries of scientific study. And thirdly, they do not incorporate the *holistic* view of the individual as a total person. They only look at people's roles within the organ- isation, failing to recognise the need and potential for individual, right-brain creative thought.

These deficiencies are all symptoms of Western society's narrow, rational, left-brain bias. Companies have to start making way for a new breed of free-thinking executives, whatever the present structure and prevailing culture. Man- agement development programmes have to incorporate right-brain techniques for problem-solving, time manage- ment and other managerial responsibilities.

Making room for creativity

The Du Pont Center for Creativity in North Carolina, USA, has recognised the need for creativity in their managers. Some of the characteristics that David Tanner, at the Cen- ter, has identified in creative thinkers are close to the right- brain traits I have seen in many top British managers:

- They have an absolute discontent with the status quo.

- They seek alternative solutions to problems or opportunities.
- They have prepared minds, being alert to things that might trigger ideas.
- They think positively, and they work hard thinking positively.

Tanner says: 'A lot of people call people who desire to change things troublemakers, but I think we need more troublemakers.'

Over the years creativity training has fallen in and out of favour with the business world. Alex F. Osborn was an early proponent. In 1942 he wrote the first serious book on creativity, *How to Think Up*, which really opened people's eyes to the fact that you could do something deliberate to stimulate creativity – namely, train the individual. Edward de Bono, the originator of Lateral Thinking, has repeated the message eloquently. More recent developments in Neuro-Linguistic Programming, sometimes called the science of personal excellence, leave us in no doubt that you as an individual can take control of your natural, creative power. In the light of new thinking technology, present improbabilities can become possibilities for achieving career and life goals. And the changes in you are bound to affect your organisation.

As a new kind of manager, able to deal with any degree of environmental change and turbulence, you are the link between personal excellence and a re-invented corporation, where people come first. Although, by its very nature, personal creativity cannot be institutionalised, and is not amenable to the neat corporate models to which we have become accustomed, it has to be identified and understood as a phenomenon – as a learnable process. It is the hallmark of Manager 2000 in a corporate setting. It is the holistic view of the individual that opens up untold possibilities. Start to see yourself as more than an institutional resource, a corporate chattel. You are a unique person with unimaginable

171

(which you now know means imaginable), realisable, creative potential. Using the untapped resources of the right-brain hemisphere, you can begin to create your own better future, inside or outside a company.

Personal excellence

A thread of personal excellence, of natural and irrepressible human creativity, runs through the fabric of any corporate or organisational achievement. You not only have personal title to the untapped ocean of your mind, but you have the natural ability to explore its depths and enjoy its treasures. You are equal to any management guru who has stumbled on a few insights.

In their book, *In Search of Excellence*, Tom Peters and Robert Waterman identified two of the major characteristics of successful companies:

- Autonomy and entrepreneurship. Leaders and individual innovators are respected and fostered. Champions are needed – for products, for ideas, for change. Risk-taking is positively encouraged.
- Values. The basic values and philosophies of an organisation have far more to do with its achievements than do technological or economic resources. Strongly held beliefs mark the successful companies.

Leaders with a vision

Peters and Waterman began by discounting the role of leadership in corporate success:

Our strongly held belief was that the excellent companies had gotten to be the way they are because of a unique set of cultural attributes that distinguish them from the rest, and if we understood those attributes well enough we could do more than just mutter 'leadership' in response to questions like 'Why is J & J so good?'

In fact they found that associated with almost every excellent company was a strong leader (or two) who seemed to have a lot to do with making the company excellent in the first place. 'Many of these companies . . . seem to have taken on their basic character under the tutelage of a *very special person*. Moreover they did it at a fairly early stage in their development.'

So it seemed to boil down to visionary leadership. The importance of the individual was clear. And they then observed that the excellent companies seemed to have developed cultures that incorporated the values and practices of the great leaders, and those shared values could thus survive for decades after the passing of the original guru. So what at first glance appears to be a cultural feature, can usually be traced back to a visionary thinker and leader whose influence outlives his organisational role. And these visionary thinkers walked and talked more like right-brain entrepreneurs than left-brain professional managers.

Unfortunately *In Search of Excellence*, although recognising such personal contributions, majored on *corporate* success criteria, such as strategy, systems and skills, and made them fit into a neat model. The recent demise of several of the 'successful' companies further supports the idea that the focus should be personal rather than organisational.

One feature of personal vision is the ability to extract extraordinary contributions from a lot of people. And this ability is not derived from applying an authoritarian or consensus style of management, or adopting a centralised or decentralised structure, or even from a thorough understanding of motivation theory. The ability comes from the personal vision, the purpose, the dream that is big enough and clear enough to be shared. Such a person is a leader, not because he or she leads, but because people tend to follow.

Henry Mintzberg, a household name in management science, states the right-brain case:

> *One fact recurs repeatedly in all of this research: the key managerial processes are enormously complex and mysterious (to me as a researcher, as well as to the managers who carry them out), drawing on the vaguest of information and using the least articulated mental processes. These processes seem to be more relational and holistic than ordered and sequential, and more intuitive than intellectual;* ***they seem to be most characteristic of right-hemispheric activity*** *[my emphasis].*

Here is the point for you and me. These 'great' leaders only appear great with hindsight. Their greatness started with a crazy notion, a purpose, some unnoticed seedling of an idea, a dream. They simply did not follow the rational rule book.

When interviewing top chief executives in the UK I tried to trace common features in those that were 'right of centre' in their thinking style – that is, they used intuition, insight and imagination and were wary of analytical methods. No common features seemed to emerge. The intuitive insights, for instance, would happen in different ways and at different times. Some executives would always share ideas with colleagues, whilst others would trust their judgement without going through a consensus process. Others would painstakingly verify their right-brain judgement with analysis and back-up – which others openly scorned as worthless. Some would make instant people decisions, whilst others would allow their feelings plenty of time to become clear. But one right-brain feature was common to all of them: the ability to envision the future, to imagine different scenarios. And this is the visionary quality so vital to corporate leadership.

As we have seen, this visualising ability is neither a hereditary talent, nor some clever magic reserved for special people. It is the way we naturally think when we use our imagination; when we give the suppressed right brain its creative freedom. We have also seen that you can re-learn any lost thinking skill – you can *become* a visionary, a leader who can see where you and your organisation are going.

In their book *Re-inventing the Corporation*, John Naisbitt and Patricia Aburdene identified two crucial elements for social change: new values, and economic necessity. Many values changed in the sixties, and personnel and management theories reflected the general swing towards the importance of the individual. But these theories hardly penetrated the everyday life of the business community, and particularly the ever-growing multinational corporations. Douglas McGregor's Theory Y, which in effect said that people would behave better, be more productive, if they were treated with respect, was many years ahead of its time. Naisbitt makes the point that it has taken more recent economic necessity as well as the value changes of the sixties to start the real process of change. Corporate hierarchies were as entrenched and impervious to change as social institutions of any kind. Now, at last, the change is taking place, from the grass roots of individual, self-developing managers, rather than as a product of structural rationalisation or published mission statements.

The downside of all this is that we cannot model a corporate, collective gut. Companies do not have insights – people do. The good news, however, is that individual creativity and innovation is learnable, and it is possible to cultivate these natural but suppressed characteristics within the corporation at every level. Only the down-valued intuitive leap can match the complex problems we all face. The search for corporate excellence has become the search for personal excellence. And the search for personal excellence has become the search of tomorrow's right-brain manager.

A new kind of manager

Manager 2000 will be able to see from other, new perspectives without losing the rational left-brain view. That is, he or she will have a balanced, multi-faceted or holistic view of what is going on – a way of thinking which harnesses the whole brain. Harold Leavitt of Stanford University, USA, sees the management process as an interactive flow of three variables:

- Pathfinding
- Decision-making
- Implementation

The problem with the rational left-brain model is that it only addresses the middle element – decision-making.

Leavitt classified various occupations into the three categories. People who fall into the decision-making category include systems analysts, engineers, MBAs, statisticians, and – wait for it – professional managers; strange bedfellows, but alike in their bias towards the left-brain rational approach. Implementation is the right-brain 'people' end of the process, which includes selling. Similarly, the pathfinding function is essentially an aesthetic, intuitive, right-brain, design process, alien to our education and management training. In fact we need to *combine* all these elements of the management process, rather than adopt and abandon them as theoretical fashion dictates. And for the next decade at least, we need to swing away from the predominantly rational, decision-making part of the process, just to redress the balance.

As a pathfinder you will see where you want to be and inspire others to go along with you. As an implementer you will have to 'sell' what is patently obvious, and analytically proven. In both roles you will need to take people with you. People are not interested in other people's babies – only in their own babies. They have to believe in something – out of free choice rather than as a handed-down corporate mission statement. And so too for your fellow-managers. People don't rally round a sound analysis or spreadsheet. They follow a person. So the rational model which excluded personal vision and initiative, whilst not dead, has to be made to lie down for a while.

This is a bitter pill for the manager who has always embraced scientific method. After all, it has taken many years to win the term 'management science'. But science itself is straining at the seams of its rational model. The typical scientific paper reproduces few of the false starts, intuitive leaps, loose ends and happy accidents that all scientists are familiar with. At worst, because of our different personal perceptions (from which no scientist is immune), they can, unwittingly or otherwise, distort the very 'objective truth' they purport to uphold. Narrow, left-brain thinking is no longer an impregnable refuge. Things no longer happen according to plan, and are not reducible to tidy little models or theories. So we need a new kind of manager – a leader with enough creativity to match the pace of change, adept at posing new questions rather than stock-piling old answers.

In the recent classic *On Becoming a Leader*, Warren Bennis's ingredients for a modern-day leader include:

- A guiding vision
- Passion
- Integrity
- Trust
- Curiosity and daring

These are not the traditional management textbook traits. Where is the control and planning, where is the analysis and rational decision-making, and where is 'the bottom line'?

Tomorrow's manager will be a leader, in ideas, in influence, if not in the old hierarchical sense. But whatever the title, the new role of the manager is gradually becoming clear. The distinctions Bennis makes between managers and leaders simply help to identify Manager 2000.

Rate yourself as a leader

Bennis's list, below, shows the left-brain skills traditionally used by managers and the right-brain qualities associated with leaders. You may wish to use the list to rate yourself as a leader/manager:

- The manager administers; the leader innovates.
- The manager focuses on systems and structure; the leader focuses on people.
- The manager has a short-range view; the leader has a long-range perspective.
- The manager has his eye on the bottom line; the leader has his eye on the horizon.
- The manager imitates; the leader originates.
- The manager accepts the status quo; the leader challenges it.
- The manager is the classic good soldier; the leader is his own person.

To become a real manager then, you must become yourself, and express these right-brain leadership qualities. However you rated on Bennis's list, change is within your power.

The time for a new kind of leader-manager is long overdue. A cursory historical review of management knowledge and practice over several decades shows that professional management has never come of age. We have accrued a handful of theories, each slowly replacing the other as managerial fashion has changed. We have yet to bring together the different pieces of the jigsaw.

The nine-minute manager

It took Henry Mintzberg, after rigorous research, to tell us what we always knew; that what the textbooks said did not happen in practice. Managers did not rationally 'analyse, plan, decide, and monitor'. Instead, they were very human, reactive, fire fighting products of a changing, seemingly unmanageable world of business. Rather than allocating large chunks of time to important tasks, as the time management books instructed, the average time a manager devoted to any one issue was *nine minutes*. What managers *should* do was light years away from what they *did* do. So much for the myth that well-trained professional managers could manage anything, that detached, analytical decision-making was the way to excellence; that what the left brain *thought* it could do it actually did.

All this is now well known, and blame has been spread widely. Tom Peters makes a damning attack on American business in his bestseller *Thriving on Chaos*. No European observer would claim that the UK is free of a similar managerial malaise, although economic events on each side of the Atlantic suggest different causes. Business schools have taken a hammering. A *New York Times* article pinpointed the MBA (Master of Business Administration degree) as part of the problem – biased as it has traditionally been towards numeracy and analysis. The most accurate diagnoses seem to be those which identify a left-brain dominance, an obsessive concern with numbers and analysis at the expense of vision, imagination and the ability to innovate in a changing environment.

Business leaders with a proven track record of achievement voice their opinions:

'So-called professional managers lack the right perspective.'

'. . . they need a broader vision.'

'most top management is lacking a gut feeling. . .'

'the majority of businessmen are incapable of original thought because they are unable to escape the tyranny of reason.'

Many eminent management thinkers and practitioners are beginning to tell the same story, and even the business schools are switching away from theory to organisation-based action learning MBAs. All this heralds a new kind of manager.

The big change to come

Thomas Khun, in identifying the major advances in science, refers to the 'paradigm shift'. Such a shift gave us the theories of relativity in physics and plate tectonics in geology. Sooner or later the orthodoxy of rationality has to be replaced by something altogether new and different. And it starts with the way we think.

In the context of what has been going on around us in some branches of science and technology, how far has management moved? We have been centralised then de-centralised at the pace of a slow pendulum. We have gone through 'big is beautiful', when economy of scale laws ruled, to the 'small is beautiful' and 'stick to the knitting' cults that followed diversification catastrophes. But where is the managerial leap forward to compare with quantum mechanics in physics, or the silicon chip in the information and communications industry?

The truth is that advances in management theory and practice have not kept pace with the staggering changes that have been going on around us. Even more worryingly, any important advances have not emerged from within the ranks of practising managers, nor even the mushrooming business schools, but as reactions to external events.

Some twenty-five years ago Jay Forrester wrote of a 'New Corporate Design'. His remarkable work predicted many of the changes we have seen in the last few years. He also, without addressing the issues from a psychological angle, stumbled on the need for right-brain thinking in management. 'In technology,' he said, 'we expect bold experiments that test ideas, obtain new knowledge, and lead to major advances. But in matters of social organisation, we usually propose only timid modifications of conventional practice and baulk at daring experiment and innovation. Why?'

Forrester did not answer his searching question, but he did describe his New Corporate Design. He saw the hierarchical structure where everyone has a boss and a subordinate as corrupting of the human spirit. Based on a great deal of political, economic and psychological evidence, he exposed the 'stultifying effect of the authoritarian organisation on initiative and innovation'. He envisaged a continually changing structure of relationships, freely negotiated by the individual. Clearly, individual creativity can be the basis of a strong corporate culture rather than sowing the seeds of anarchy. And some organisations are already harnessing personal vision to realise corporate ends.

Week by week, there are signs of the emergence of a new kind of corporate manager. Such a special role is not for the genetically blessed or the lucky few. It is for the ordinary manager who has learned to think in a better way, who has learned to call routinely on god-like powers of insight and creativity, whose inner subjective world can conceive objective realities and bring them about against all the odds. This person is well trained professionally, has feet firmly on the ground, and uses to the full all his or her left-brain powers when occasion demands, yet is unmistakably identified as a *right-brain manager*.

FURTHER READING

Bennis, Warren, *On Becoming a Leader* (Century Hutchinson Ltd 1989)

Buzan, Tony, *Make the Most of Your Mind* (Colt Books Ltd 1988)

De Bono, Edward, *Lateral Thinking* (Penguin Books 1977)

Edwards, Betty, *Drawing on the Right Side of the Brain* (Souvenir Press Ltd 1981)

Lorayne, Harry, *Remembering People* (Stein & Day 1975)

Maltz, Maxwell, *Psycho-cybernetics* (Simon & Schuster 1960)

O'Connor, Joseph and Seymour, John, *Introducing Neuro-linguistic Programming* (HarperCollins 1990)

Zdenek, Marilee, *The Right Brain Experience* (Transworld Publishers Ltd [Corgi] 1985)

183

INDEX

Piatkus Business Books

Piatkus Business Books have been created for people like you, busy executives and managers who need expert knowledge readily available in a clear and easy-to-follow format. All the books are written by specialists in their field. They will help you improve your skills quickly and effortlessly in the workplace and on a personal level. Titles include:

General Management Skills

Sales and Customer Services

Presentation and Communication

Better Business Writing   Maryann V. Piotrowski
The Complete Book of Business Etiquette   Lynne Brennan and
David Block
**Confident Conversation: How to Talk in any Business or Social
Situation**   Dr Lillian Glass
**Powerspeak: The Complete Guide to Public Speaking and
Presentation**   Dorothy Leeds
**The Power Talk System: How to Communicate
Effectively**   Christian H. Godefroy and Stephanie Barrat
**Personal Power: How to Achieve Influence and Success in Your
Professional Life**   Philippa Davies
Say What You Mean and Get What You Want   George R. Walther
Your Total Image: How to Communicate Success   Philippa
Davies

Careers

**The Influential Woman: How to Achieve Success Without Losing
Your Femininity**   Lee Bryce
**Marketing Yourself: How to Sell Yourself and Get the Jobs
You've Always Wanted**   Dorothy Leeds
Networking and Mentoring: A Woman's Guide   Dr Lily
Segerman-Peck
**Which Way Now? How to Plan and Develop a Successful
Career**   Bridget Wright
The Perfect CV: How to Get the Job You Really Want   Tom
Jackson
Ten Steps to the Top   Marie Jennings

Small Business

**The Best Person for the Job: Where to Find Them and How to
Keep Them**   Malcolm Bird
How to Collect the Money You Are Owed   Malcolm Bird
**Making Profits: A Six-Month Plan for the Small
Business**   Malcolm Bird
Organize Yourself   Ronni Eisenberg and Kate Kelly

For a free brochure with further information on our complete
range of business titles, please write to:

**Piatkus Books
Freepost 7 (WD 4505)
London W1E 4EZ**

PIATKUS

Sales Power
by José Silva and Ed Bernd Jnr

The revolutionary Silva Method is the world's fastest
growing and most successful personal development system.
Sales Power offers simple, proven techniques which you can
use to unlock the hidden potential of your mind and
increase your sales and income. Use it to:

- Prospect more effectively
- Establish rapport with your prospect
- Handle objections smoothly, confidently and easily
- Attain and exceed sales goals and quotas

José Silva is the founder of The Silva Method, the world's
most famous mind development training programme, and
author of books totalling more than 1,000,000 copies in
print.

The Complete Time Management System
by Christian H. Godefroy and John Clark

The Complete Time Management System will change the
way you work and think. It is packed with easy and effective
strategies designed to help you succeed. It will show you:

- How to do in 2 hours what you usually need 4 hours to
  do
- How to read 240 pages an hour – with better
  understanding and memorization
- How to make an important decision faster
- How to delegate
- How to organize your office

Learn the secrets of time management and you will profit
from them all your life.

Christian H. Godefroy is a training specialist, author and
founder of a publishing company in France. His co-author
John Clark is a management consultant.

Quantum Learning
by Bobbi DePorter with Mike Hernacki

Quantum Learning provides clear exercises, tips and strategies for success that can make anybody a winner in the classroom, in a career, and in life. You will learn:

- How to master effective note-taking techniques
- How to discover your own personal learning style
- How to cultivate a winning attitude
- How to work your own memory miracles
- How to write with confidence

Bobbi DePorter is an expert in accelerated learning. She runs SuperCamp, a college which provides learning-how-to-learn techniques to students in the United States and around the world. Mike Hernacki is a former teacher and attorney, and author of several books.

Mind Power
by Christian H. Godefroy

Mind Power will help you achieve the good things in life by showing you how to harness the extraordinary power of your subconscious mind. Use this simple technique to:

- Make positive changes in your life
- Boost your self-confidence and self-esteem
- Develop an excellent memory and increase your creativity
- Become healthy and strengthen your immune system
- Control bad habits – and stop yourself from smoking!

Christian Godefroy is a specialist in positive thinking and the author of several bestselling books.

Memory Booster
by Robert W. Finkel

Memory Booster is the key to improving your memory and increasing your brainpower. It contains step-by-step techniques which will help you to learn faster and memorise more than you ever thought possible. You will discover dozens of easy ways to remember:

- Everything you read, in detail
- Words, terms and foreign languages
- Telephone numbers, prices and dates
- Up to a dozen names, after a single introduction
- Diagrams, processes and facts

Robert Finkel PhD is a theoretical physicist and chairman of the department of physics at St John's University, New York. He is a consultant to industry and the US government.

Brain Power
by Marilyn vos Savant and Leonore Fleischer

This unique 12-week mental training programme will show you how to:

- Build the power and capacity of your brain and intelligence
- Increase your vocabulary
- Strengthen your attention span and your senses
- Develop a logical mind
- Accept challenges and solve problems
- Improve your powers of reasoning and comprehension
- Expand your viewpoint
- Realise your full potential and live life to the full

You don't need a degree to improve your brain power – you just need determination and this book.

Marilyn vos Savant has an IQ of 230, the highest IQ ever measured (the average is 100). She lectures on mental training to universities and businesses.